Cambridge Elements

Elements in Cognitive Linguistics
edited by
Sarah Duffy
Northumbria University
Nick Riches
Newcastle University

CREATIVE CONSTRUCTION GRAMMAR

Thomas Hoffmann
KU Eichstätt-Ingolstadt

Mark Turner
Case Western Reserve University

Shaftesbury Road, Cambridge CB2 8EA, United Kingdom

One Liberty Plaza, 20th Floor, New York, NY 10006, USA

477 Williamstown Road, Port Melbourne, VIC 3207, Australia

314–321, 3rd Floor, Plot 3, Splendor Forum, Jasola District Centre,
New Delhi – 110025, India

103 Penang Road, #05–06/07, Visioncrest Commercial, Singapore 238467

Cambridge University Press is part of Cambridge University Press & Assessment,
a department of the University of Cambridge.

We share the University's mission to contribute to society through the pursuit of
education, learning and research at the highest international levels of excellence.

www.cambridge.org
Information on this title: www.cambridge.org/9781009635271

DOI: 10.1017/9781009635240

© Thomas Hoffmann and Mark Turner 2025

This publication is in copyright. Subject to statutory exception and
to the provisions of relevant collective licensing agreements, with the exception
of the Creative Commons version the link for which is provided below, no
reproduction of any part may take place without the written permission of
Cambridge University Press & Assessment.

An online version of this work is published at doi.org/10.1017/9781009635240
under a Creative Commons Open Access license CC-BY-NC 4.0 which permits
re-use, distribution and reproduction in any medium for non-commercial purposes
providing appropriate credit to the original work is given and any changes made
are indicated. To view a copy of this license visit https://creativecommons.org/
licenses/by-nc/4.0

When citing this work, please include a reference to the
DOI 10.1017/9781009635240

First published 2025

A catalogue record for this publication is available from the British Library

*A Cataloging-in-Publication data record for this Element is available from the
Library of Congress*

ISBN 978-1-009-63525-7 Hardback
ISBN 978-1-009-63527-1 Paperback
ISSN 2633-3325 (online)
ISSN 2633-3317 (print)

Cambridge University Press & Assessment has no responsibility for the persistence
or accuracy of URLs for external or third-party internet websites referred to in this
publication and does not guarantee that any content on such websites is, or will
remain, accurate or appropriate.

For EU product safety concerns, contact us at Calle de José Abascal, 56, 1°, 28003
Madrid, Spain, or email eugpsr@cambridge.org

Creative Construction Grammar

Elements in Cognitive Linguistics

DOI: 10.1017/9781009635240
First published online: December 2025

Thomas Hoffmann
KU Eichstätt-Ingolstadt

Mark Turner
Case Western Reserve University

Author for correspondence: Thomas Hoffmann, thomas.hoffmann@ku.de

Abstract: Constructions are long-term pairings in memory of form and meaning. How are they created and learned, how do they change, and how do they combine into new utterances (constructs, communicative performances) in the working memory? Drawing on evidence from word-formation (blending, Noun–Noun compounds) over idioms and argument structure constructions to multimodal communication, we argue that computational metaphors such as 'unification' or 'constraint satisfaction' do not constitute a cognitively adequate explanation. Instead, we put forward the idea that construction formation and combination are achieved through *conceptual blending* – a domain-general process of higher cognition that has been used to explain complex human behavior such as scientific discovery, reasoning, art, music, dance, math, social cognition, and religion. This title is also available as Open Access on Cambridge Core.

Keywords: cognitive linguistics, construction grammar, cognitive science, syntax, cognition

© Thomas Hoffmann and Mark Turner 2025

ISBNs: 9781009635257 (HB), 9781009635271 (PB), 9781009635240 (OC)
ISSNs: 2633-3325 (online), 2633-3317 (print)

Contents

1 What Is 'Creative Construction Grammar'?   1

2 Why Construction Grammar Needs a Theory of Creative Combination   11

3 Candidate Theories of Creative Combination   15

4 Blending   29

5 Creative Construction Grammar: Blending in Action   52

6 Conclusion   63

    References   65

1 What Is 'Creative Construction Grammar'?

A sound is just a sound: It is a perception of longitudinal waves striking the eardrum. The sound we utter when we say 'dog' is merely a string of sounds, merely a form; it is not a dog, and it does not *intrinsically* mean *dog*. The *form* and the *meaning* are *radically different things*. But, mentally, we *pair* that form with the concept of a dog (/dɑːg/ ⇔ 'concept of a dog'). Human beings are the symbolic species (Deacon 1997): They are prone to associate forms with meanings (form ⇔ meaning). In fact, Construction Grammar (CxG) (e.g., Goldberg 2019; Hilpert 2019; Hoffmann 2022a; Ungerer & Hartmann 2024) argues that form-meaning pairings (known as 'constructions') that are stored in the long-term memory are *the* central units of language. Construction Grammar consequently investigates how we create and invent form-meaning pairs, how we combine them into utterances, and how we unpack those utterances to construct meanings. To know a communicative system is to know a relational network of constructions (Diessel 2019, 2023; Sommerer & Van de Velde 2025) and how they combine to create constructs. As a term, 'construct' denotes the mental representation of this combination process. The communicator then turns the constructs into a perceivable product that comprises the verbal utterance as well as any multimodal information such as gaze, stance, gestures, and so on. We call this a 'performance.' To construct a meaning in response to a communicative performance is to consider how the communicator could have blended the form parts of various form-meaning pairs into that performance. The mental space network built by the construer of those form-meaning pairs enables the construer to attribute a meaning to that communicative performance.

In this Element, we present our approach to Construction Grammar, which we label Creative Construction Grammar. One meaning of Creative Construction Grammar that we want to explore is the study of creative, playful, innovative uses of form-meaning pairs. Everyone notices and remarks upon such obvious creativity. Take, for example, the following instances of the well-known XYZ construction (Turner 1987; Turner & Fauconnier 1999):

(1) Amazon Is the Apex Predator of Our Platform Era (the headline of a *New York Times* article by Cory Doctorow [2023])

(2) Shortbread, the little black dress of cookies (the title of a post on the blog *bring a little bread* [Sarah Grace 2012])

(3) We don't want to be the German car industry of news publishing (Emma Thompson, the new Editor of *The Wall Street Journal*,

joking to the hundreds of staff members listening, as quoted by Katie Robertson [2023]) (Thompson was commenting on news about how German carmakers were slipping behind Tesla and China in the transition to electronic vehicles.)

(4) It is also November. The noons are more laconic and the sundowns sterner, and Gibraltar lights make the village foreign. November always seemed to me the Norway of the year.
(Emily Dickinson, in an 1864 letter to Mrs. J.G. Holland [Bianchi 1971: 259–260])

(5) XYZ is the Anax of constructions (Eve Sweetser, personal communication, August 29, 2025) ('Anax' [ἄναξ] is a word in Ancient Greek that appears in, e.g., *The Iliad*, to refer to high kings – e.g., Agamemnon and Priam – who exercise lordship over other, lesser, kings.)

We will discuss examples such as these in more detail later. For now, we just want to highlight the fabulous playfulness in these linguistic prompts: They were put together inventively, and they prompt for us to construct remarkable and unusual conceptual blends of Amazon and the lion (1), of a little black dress and a cookie (2), of the German car industry and news publishing (3), of November and Norway (4), of Anax and a clausal construction (5). This type of creative language use has recently received considerable attention in constructionist research (see, e.g., Bergs 2018, 2019; Bergs & Kompa 2020; Hartmann & Ungerer 2024; Herbst 2020; Hoffmann 2018, 2019a, 2020a, 2020b, 2022b, 2024, 2025, fc.; Trousdale 2018, 2020; Turner 2018, 2020; Uhrig 2018, 2020).

As Hoffmann (2022b, 2024, 2025, fc.) points out in his 5C model of constructional creativity, a Creative Construction Grammar that aims to analyze such striking expressions not only needs to take into account the constructional network that underlies these creative constructs. It also must pay attention to the producer (the 'constructor') and their audience (the 'co-constructors') as well as, and of central relevance to the present Element, the mental process ('constructional blending') that produces these 'creative constructs' in the working memory.

Our Creative Construction Grammar approach, however, is not limited to just such blatantly creative examples. While constructions are stored in the long-term memory, constructs are form-meaning pairings that are created in the working memory (see Hoffmann 2017a, 2022a, 2024, 2025). Only in rare cases does a construct involve a single construction (e.g., when reproducing prefabs such as "Thank you!" or "You're welcome"). Instead, more frequently, speakers will combine several constructions to create a construct. Take the examples in (6) and (7):

(6) The novice skier walked her way down the ski slope. (Goldberg 1995: 205)

(7) Stacey clawed her way to the top. (TV 2012 US/CA Masterchef)

Both of these draw on the *Way* construction (Goldberg 1995: 199–218; Israel 1996), which, simplifying somewhat, has the form [A VERB possessive_pronoun$_i$ *way* PP] and a meaning of 'A traverses the path$_{PP}$ while/by doing VERB' (for more details, see Brunner & Hoffmann 2020: 5; Hoffmann 2022a: 188). In (6), *the novice skier* is in the A slot, *her* fills the possessive pronoun slot, and *down the ski slope* is in the PP slot, leading to an interpretation of 'the novice skier traversed down the ski slope by walking.' Similarly, *Stacey*, *her*, and *to the top* combine with the *Way* construction to yield the meaning 'Stacey traversed to the top by clawing.'

(7) is arguably more creative than (6) since the former uses a non-motion verb (*claw*) while the latter has a motion verb (*walk*) in the *Way* construction. In both cases, however, we would like to raise the question of what is meant by statements such as '*the novice skier* is in/fills the A slot' or 'Stacey combines with the *Way* construction': What is the underlying cognitive process that combines constructions in the working memory? As we shall argue, metaphors such as 'merge,' 'combine,' or 'unify' do not constitute cognitively plausible processes. Instead, we will argue that the domain-general process of conceptual blending underlies the combination of more innovative constructs such as (1–5), as well as more "normal" combinations such as (6) and (7).

Finally, we will illustrate that conceptual blending is also required for all associations of forms and meanings in the working memory. This is obvious when looking at the holophrases that children produce during language acquisition. A form such as /foʊn/ (*phone*) can be used by a child to express a myriad of different meanings (here drawing on data from Tomasello's own daughter): "First used in response to hearing the telephone ring, then as she 'talked' on the phone, then to point at and name the phone, and then when she wanted someone to pick her up so she could talk on the wall-phone (pointing to it)" (Tomasello 2003: 36). Similarly, *bath* was used by Tomasello's daughter "as an accompaniment to preparations for bath, then as she bathed her baby doll" (Tomasello 2003: 37). In order to correctly understand what their children are trying to communicate with a given form, parents obviously must draw on the constructions they have stored in the long-term memory (such as /foʊn/ ⇔ 'concept of a telephone'). Yet these constructions only serve as prompts for a complex mental operation that, guided by joint attention (Tomasello 2003), allows them to guess the particular communicative intention that the child is trying to express. This type of online semiosis is typical of not only parent-child interaction. Even when adults have stored a large number of form-meaning pairs in their mental network, enabling them to produce more complex messages, the meaning pole of entrenched constructions merely provides a starting point for further elaboration. Take the form-meaning pair *tiger* (/ˈtaɪgəɹ/ ⇔ 'concept of a tiger'): As Casasanto and Lupyan (2015: 551), among others, point out, it is impossible to specify a single necessary and sufficient property that is constantly associated with a word construction. In a specific communicative situation, *tiger* might be used to refer to the actual animal (cf. *Well, Siegfried and Roy make that tiger disappear.* TV Corpus US/CA 1995 Married with Children) – but, similarly, it can also be used to talk about a toy (cf. *Give me three more balls. I'm going for that big stuffed tiger.* TV Corpus 2009 US/CA Heroes). Occasionally, it is also used to address humans (cf. *Go get them, tiger.* TV Corpus 1998 US/CA Full House).[1] As we will argue, what is therefore also needed in Construction Grammar is a cognitive operation that enables humans to produce and understand the dynamic form-meaning associations that are created on the fly in the working memory for a specific communicative act.

Importantly, however, we do not claim that conceptual blending is the single cognitive operation that renders all other processes obsolete. In line with Usage-based Construction Grammar approaches (cf., e.g., Bybee 2006, 2010, 2013; Croft 2001; Diessel 2019; Goldberg 2006, 2019), we maintain that the mental constructicon of speakers is shaped by the repeated exposure to specific utterances (i.e., constructs) and that domain-general cognitive processes such as analogy, categorization, chunking, or cross-modal association play a crucial role in the mental entrenchment of constructions. Entrenchment is a metaphor for the storage of information in the long-term memory (the strengthening of associations and their routinization;

---

[1] An anonymous reviewer raised the question whether this is merely a case of polysemy. This would imply that all the above uses of *tiger* are stored as separate but related concepts. We side with Casasanto & Lupyan (2015), however, that meanings are not statically stored but dynamically created during use. Words and constructions in this approach are prompts for dynamic meaning-making in context. Note that this view also goes beyond analyses that assume pragmatic enrichment in which stable semantic meanings are enriched during language use. For fuller discussion, see Fauconnier & Turner (2003).

Schmid 2020) and we subscribe to Goldberg's (2019) definition, which states that

> constructions are understood to be emergent clusters of lossy memory traces that are aligned within our high- (hyper!) dimensional conceptual space on the basis of shared form, function, and contextual dimensions. (Goldberg 2019: 7)

Whenever we combine constructions into constructs, however, we must not only activate these associations in the working memory to produce them; in line with recent work in cognitive psychology, we "conceive of working memory as *attentional processes* operating on *long-term memory*" (Schweppe & Rummer 2014: 286). As we will show in this Element, humans do not compositionally combine constructions they combine them in a way that is best modeled by conceptual blending. Once a construct is uttered it becomes a token of usage and can consequently become entrenched in the long-term memory. The process of initial combination, however, will involve information activated in the working memory.[2]

Creative Construction Grammar, therefore, aims to account for communicative performances that are considered 'creative' as well as 'normal uses' of language that do not strike people as particularly creative. As Gibbs has pointed out, routine language draws on "many of the same mental/linguistic routines employed in creative language use" (2025: 43; cf. also Gibbs 2018). Experiments show that even when processing conventional metaphors (such as *We have really come a long way since the wedding*; Gibbs 2017), speakers recruit cross-domain mappings (Gibbs 2025: 49). The real difference between 'creative' and 'routine' uses of language lies in the degree to which speakers are consciously aware of a communicative performance: "[S]o-called automatic behavior is really organized by a complex set of cognitive, perceptual, and motor skills, all of which operate again without much conscious awareness" (Gibbs 2018).

---

[2] It is important to note that the neurological processes underlying all of these processes are still not fully understood. Neuroscientific creativity research standardly distinguishes a generation phase and an evaluation phase (cf., e.g., Kleinmintz, Ivancovsky & Shamay-Tsoory 2019). Recently, Ovando-Tellez et al. (2022) found that divergent thinking involves the interaction of the executive control network and salience and attentional brain regions, while convergent thinking draws on the connectivity between the default mode and control and salience network of the brain. Conceptual blending obviously combines elements of the generation phase as well as the evaluation phase. Much more research will be necessary to map the claims of Creative Construction Grammar onto neuroscientific studies. The current Element prioritizes establishing conceptual blending as the cognitive domain-general mechanism of constructional combination. Future neuroscientific research can then use the insights of this proposal to test it in empirical studies.

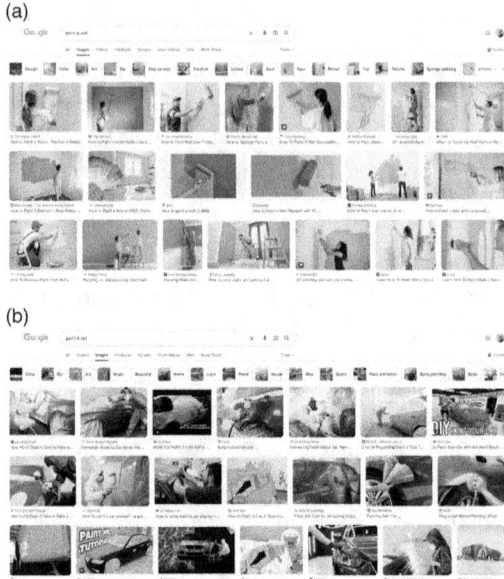

Figure 1 (a) Top Google image search result for 'paint a wall' and (b) top Google image search result for 'paint a car.'

Sometimes these complex processes only become apparent when comparing two seemingly similar, 'simple' utterances. Take the statements *The man painted the wall black* versus *The man painted the car black*.[3] Despite the superficial similarity of the two utterances, the events that are mentally conjured up when processing them differ considerably with respect to type of paint and tools, as well as choice of clothes. The results of the respective Google image searches shown in Figure 1 are a case in point.

Search engine results do not, of course, constitute evidence for mental processes. The images in Figure 1 do, however, illustrate crucially different prototypical associations of apparently 'compositional' utterances of the type *X paints Y*.

In this Element, we argue that *any* discussion of constructions and communicative performances fundamentally depends on a theory of creative combination. A theory of creative combination is the indispensable heart of Construction Grammar. But surprisingly, so far Construction Grammar does not offer such a theory: It has a gaping hole where its heart should be. The central claim of this Element is that the best candidate for

---

[3] An anonymous reviewer raised the issue covered in this paragraph by asking how conceptual blending was involved in processing "such relatively uncreative language use." As Figure 1 shows, even apparently uncreative uses require considerable frame blending.

a theory of creative construction combination is the theory of Conceptual Integration, also known as 'Blending' (Fauconnier & Turner 2002).

Blending is a domain-general cognitive process that takes two or more inputs (e.g., semantic frames, words, constructions, gestures, images, ideas, etc.) and combines them into a blend. This process is selective (not every detail from an input space appears in the blend) and frequently gives rise to emergent meanings (which are not part of any of the input spaces). In the history of philology, rhetoric, and linguistics, there were many efforts to account for what looked like pyrotechnic special cases, such as remarkable metaphors, metonymies, analogies, and so on. In this Element, by contrast, we put forward the claim that blending is a domain-general process, and we argue that it is the central, indispensable process for all communication, including even the most basic cases. The present Element cannot provide a self-contained, expert presentation of every detail of blending theory (for this, see book-length treatments such as Fauconnier & Turner 2002 or Turner 2014). We do, however, present ample evidence for our main claim Section 2 will elaborate on why we think Construction Grammar needs blending as its theory of construction combination, and Section 4 will show how blending theory meets the requirements of constructional combination. In the remainder of this section, we will shortly survey the evidence that blending is a domain-general cognitive process.

Conceptual blending is not at all specific to language. Quite the contrary. Conceptual blending is a domain-general process whose workings have been extensively examined in art, music, religion, mathematical insight, scientific discovery, advanced social cognition, advanced tool invention, fashion, and so on (Fauconnier & Turner, 2002; Turner 2014). The great majority of research on blending lies outside the field of linguistics. Consider the invention of non-Euclidean geometry (Turner 2001), which began from attempts to derive rather than assume the parallel axiom. So many geometers, regarding the parallel axiom as an embarrassment, had tried and failed to prove (rather than assume) the parallel axiom that as early as 1767, Jean le Rond d'Alembert (1717–1783) referred to it as "the scandal of the elements of geometry" (1767: 203–207). Gerolamo Saccheri (1667–1733) made a remarkable attempt that focused on a quadrilateral $ABCD$ where $<DAB$ and $<ABC$ are right angles, and where line segments $\overline{AD}$ and $\overline{BC}$ are equal. Without using the parallel axiom, it is easy to prove that $<BCD$ and $<CDA$ must be equal angles. Saccheri did this. If we assume the parallel axiom, $<BCD$ and $<CDA$ can be proven to be right angles. (In fact, the implication works in both directions: The parallel axiom is equivalent to the

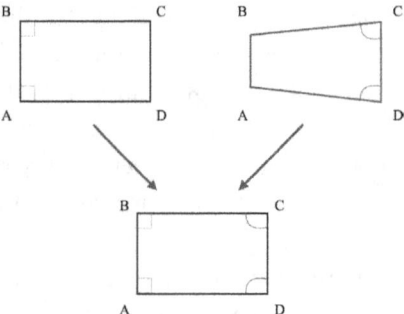

Figure 2 Blending analysis of Saccheri's quadrilateral

assumption that <BCD and <CDA are right angles. But all we need for this analysis is the first direction, i.e., that the parallel axiom implies that <BCD and <CDA are right angles.) Therefore, if we deny that <BCD and <CDA are right angles, we thereby deny the parallel axiom. Saccheri did just this in the hope of deriving a contradiction from the denial, which would prove the parallel axiom by *reductio ad absurdum*. But if <BCD and <CDA are not right angles, they are still equal, and so they must be either obtuse or acute. Saccheri attempted to show that, in either case, a contradiction follows. He assumed that they are acute; that is, he proposed a conceptual blend of two routine Euclidean figures. Both have a quadrilateral $ABCD$, equal line segments $\overline{AD}$ and $\overline{BC}$, equal angles <DAB and <ABC, and equal angles <BCD and <CDA. The blend takes this structure from both inputs. But the first input has right internal angles <DAB and <ABC, and the second input has acute internal angles <BCD and <CDA. The blend takes the right angles from the first input and the acute angles from the second (see Figure 2).

The blend is impossible in Euclidean geometry, but Saccheri never found a contradiction for it. In fact, he produced many astonishing theorems that are now recognized as belonging to hyperbolic geometry. These theorems were so repugnant to commonsense notions that he concluded they must be rejected. It is important to see that all of Saccheri's elaboration of the blend followed everyday procedures of Euclidean geometry. The input spaces are Euclidean and familiar; the elaboration procedures are Euclidean and familiar. The only new thing in the process is the selective, two-sided projection to create the blend. Another theorem of Saccheri's relied on a blend having to do with parallel lines: Given any point A and a line b, there exist in the pencil (family) of lines through A two lines p and q that divide the pencil into two parts. The first of these two parts consists of the lines that intersect b, and the second consists of those lines (lying in angle α) that have a common perpendicular with b somewhere along b (see Figure 3).

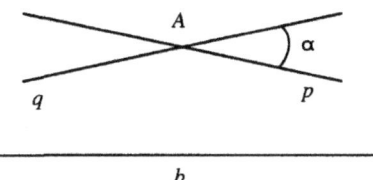

Figure 3 Saccheri's blend, in which, through a point outside a line, there is an infinity of parallel lines

The lines p and q themselves are asymptotic to b. In Euclidean geometry, angle α is 0 and p and q are identical. But for Saccheri's new geometry, derived from the acute-angle blend, angle α is positive and p and q are distinct, so that there is an infinity of lines through A that have a common perpendicular with b and never meet it. This is a blend of two standard notions: The first is a schema of a parallel line through a point outside a line; the second is a schema of a bundle of lines through a point. If we blend these, we have multiple lines through a point outside a line that are all parallel to the line.

Saccheri is not credited with the invention of non-Euclidean geometry. Credit is given instead to Gauss, Bolyai, and Lobatchevsky for recognizing (but not proving) that hyperbolic non-Euclidean geometry is mathematically consistent, and to Gauss for recognizing that physical space might be non-Euclidean. For us, today, non-Euclidean geometry is indispensable to science. We must use it, for example, to compute how to land a craft on Mars. The theory of general relativity is fundamentally built upon non-Euclidean geometry. Non-Euclidean geometry, particularly Riemannian geometry, which generalizes to curved spaces, provides the necessary mathematical tools to describe the motion of planets around stars, the bending of light around massive objects (gravitational lensing), and the behavior of objects near black holes. The operation of conceptual blending in mathematics is pervasive. It is extensively studied in Alexander 2011, Lakoff & Núñez 2000, Núñez in preparation, Steen & Turner 2025, and Turner 2019.

Blending is often introduced through such highly visible, pyrotechnic examples for the sake of pedagogy. But using flashy examples is profoundly misleading, as nearly all conceptual blending goes completely unnoticed in consciousness. By contrast, the cyclic day provides an example where the blending is still visible, but typically only once it has been pointed out. An actual day is an experience, and we can think of days as events along a timeline. That is already impressive blending: Days do not lie upon a line, nor do we move along a line through them (see Fauconnier & Turner 2008 for an analysis of the role of blending in conceiving of time). Further blending compresses a sequence of individual days into *the cyclic day*. The analogies across the inputs are compressed to identity (*the* cyclic day) and the differences are compressed to change. Now, in the blend, but not in the inputs, there is the amazing emergent structure that the day *repeats*. This conceptual blend simplifies navigation through daily routines, cultural practices, and societal structures.

The site at http://blending.stanford.edu cites many hundreds of such studies of conceptual blending in cognitive science, psychology, neuroscience, psychotherapy, mathematics, physics, political science, education, film, pretend play, religion, artificial intelligence, computation, modeling, data science, gesture, music, painting, comics, counterfactual thinking, reasoning, logic, inference, and many other fields outside of linguistics and the study of communication.

There have also been studies on the extent to which the mental operation of blending is available to other species, such as the special panel on 'Conceptual Blending in Animal Cognition' at the conference of the Cognitive Science Society held in Vienna on July 26–29, 2021 (https://youtu.be/aPpmCX0Tl7w). We emphasize that our purpose here is to analyze *cognitive processes*, not to establish definitions (such as a definition of blending). Many operations of integration have been studied in neuroscience (e.g., sensory, perceptual, time-space collocation, object permanence). Efforts to stipulate which of these count as 'blending' are merely definitional attempts: provisionally useful for this or that conversation if properly done, but not scientifically fundamental. Blending theory has usually paid attention to cases where the inputs to the blend are in conflict and the blend contains emergent structure, because these are the kinds of integration for which human beings show constant, robust, perhaps unique capacities. These are the kinds of blending for which any linguist who proposes a theory of language must account.

We turn now from blending as a general mental operation to its role in robust human communication. Turner (1996, chapter 8, 'Language') argued that cognitive operations whose existence we must grant independent of any analysis of grammar can account for the origin of grammar, and specifically that language is a byproduct of our capacity for advanced conceptual blending. As he put it, "Language follows from these mental capacities as a consequence; it is their complex product." Beate Hampe & Doris Schönefeld (2003) concur: After critiquing other approaches in the theory of Construction Grammar to account for constructions and their combinations into constructs, they write, "let us turn next to the model of 'conceptual blending,' developed by Fauconnier & Turner (1995, 1996, 1998), which we take to be the most plausible model available."

The rest of this Element argues that construction formation and construction combination are consequences of conceptual blending, a basic, domain-general mental operation in human beings. Blending theory is the basis of Construction Grammar.

2 Why Construction Grammar Needs a Theory of Creative Combination

All theories of Construction Grammar (CxG) are based on the view that human beings can create and learn form-meaning pairs (constructions) and can combine these form-meaning pairs to create more complicated expressions (Diessel 2019; Goldberg 2019; Hilpert 2019; Hoffmann 2022a; Hoffmann & Trousdale 2013; Ungerer & Hartmann 2023). For example, words are form-meaning pairs, and we can combine words to make sentences. Take the following example (from Hoffmann 2018: 264):

(8) Firefighters cut the man free
(BNC W_newsp_other_report K55)

(8) clearly comprises the words *firefighters*, *cut*, *the*, *man*, and *free*. But how exactly are these words combined into this expression? A standard assumption in CxG is that so-called argument structure constructions provide a schematic skeleton into which words (and phrases, as will be seen) can be inserted. In (8), *cut* does not just have its prototypical transitive meaning (of a 'cutter' cutting something). Instead, it is understood that *the man* ends up being free because of the cutting event, and whatever is cut (most likely a vehicle of sorts that the man was trapped in) is not even mentioned in (8) (Goldberg 1995; Fauconnier & Turner 1996). The construction that evokes this interpretation is the Resultative construction:

(9) FORM: [SBJ$_1$ V$_2$ OBJ$_3$ OBL$_4$]$_{\text{Resultative Construction}}$5
⇔
MEANING: 'A$_1$ CAUSES B$_3$ TO BECOME C$_4$ BY V$_2$-ing'
(Hoffmann 2022a: 7)

Yet how precisely does the combination of the words and the construction in (9) work? Which cognitive mechanism is supposed to account for the combination of form-meaning pairings? For centuries, linguistic approaches assumed that we combine words according to independent and meaningless syntactic rules. Construction Grammar (Hoffmann & Trousdale 2013; Hilpert 2019; Hoffmann 2022a), however, rejects this assumption.

In CxG, there are essentially two approaches to how the combination of constructions is perceived to work (for further detail on the various approaches see Hoffmann 2017b, 2022a: 258–266; Ungerer & Hartmann 2023: 22–27). First, there are formalist and computational approaches, such as Berkeley Construction Grammar (Fillmore 1985, 1988; Fillmore, Kay & O'Connor 1988; Fillmore & Kay 1993, 1995; Michaelis 1994; Michaelis & Lambrecht 1996; Fillmore 2013), Sign-based Construction Grammar (Michaelis 2010, 2013; Boas & Sag 2012), Fluid Construction Grammar (Steels 2011, 2013; van Trijp 2014), and Embodied Construction Grammar (Bergen & Chang 2005, 2013). These approaches model construction combination by either 'unification' or 'constraint satisfaction'. Yet while these mechanisms have proved very powerful in modeling language production, hardly any Construction Grammarian would claim that unification or constraint satisfaction are basic, domain-general mental operations.

On the other hand, Cognitive CxG (Croft 2001; Goldberg 2006, 2019; Boas 2013), due to its cognitive linguistic foundations, follows the axiom that linguists should "strive to account for language in terms of *more general cognition* before they posit language-dedicated cognitive capacities" (Enfield 2017: 13). As Schmid (2010: 117) observes, "[O]ne of the basic tenets of Cognitive Linguistics is that the human capacity to process language is closely linked with, perhaps even determined by, other fundamental cognitive abilities." But when it comes to how exactly constructions are supposed to combine, Cognitive CxG has not so far pointed to a specific domain-general process. Its explanations remain vague: "Allowing constructions to combine freely as long as there are no conflicts, allows for the infinitely creative potential of language" (Goldberg 2006: 22).

Goldberg (1995: 50; 2006: 39–40) (see also Boas 2013: 237–238) does, of course, outline some principles that mediate the combination of words and argument structure constructions (namely, the Semantic Coherence Principle or the Correspondence Principle). In current work, these are subsumed under the idea of 'coverage' (Goldberg 2019, discussed later) the idea that novel expressions are licensed to "the extent that the existing combination of constructions covers the hyperdimensional space required to include the novel expression" (Goldberg 2019: 73). While previously observed combinations certainly guide how we construct novel utterances, the question remains how these existing constructions were combined in the first place. In addition to the notion of coverage, however, Cognitive CxG has no specified (domain-general) process that is supposed to license the combination of constructions.

Adopting a cognitive linguistic perspective, the overarching question we ask in this Element is how exactly do speakers combine constructions in their minds? Do they simply 'additively combine' constructions? Do they 'merge' or 'unify' them? In other words, is there a domain-specific process that is involved? Most usage-based approaches maintain that CxG, as a cognitive theory of language, has a commitment to look for general cognitive operations to account for language acquisition, variation, and change. Only as a last resort should it hypothesize mental powers that operate only in the domain of language. But is there a domain-general process that could account for construction combination and is there, perhaps, also empirical evidence that such a process is actually at work?

One powerful domain-general process of higher cognition that has been shown to combine mental inputs into novel structures is Conceptual Integration, also known as conceptual blending (Turner & Fauconnier 1999). As mentioned in Section 1, conceptual blending has been used to explain complex human behaviors such as scientific discovery, reasoning, art, music, dance, social cognition, and religion. Blending theory surveys how various species possess rudimentary capacities for conceptual combination and proposes that advanced conceptual blending of the kinds that human beings can perform is perhaps only a slight advance along the cline of the basic blending operations. However, it is this advance that makes all the difference and evolutionarily permits the precipitation of a host of related creative abilities (Fauconnier & Turner 2002). While non-human species are astoundingly good at many performances at which human beings are poor, human beings show a remarkable aptitude for creative combination. Speculation about evolution aside (and examining only extant animals), we see at present great differences in creative performance between human beings and other species. Blending theory proposes that a species-wide mental operation (involving advanced forms of blending, with principles and constraints) makes all of these performances possible.

Take the example in (8): As has been mentioned, one might intuitively think that the various word constructions are merely filling in the slots of the Resultative construction (9). But the particular construal evoked by (8) goes beyond the meaning of the argument structure construction and illustrates that things are slightly more complicated: *Free* can, obviously, also mean 'free from oppression', but the selected meaning in (8) is 'free from being stuck in a crashed car'. Moreover, prototypically, firefighters fight fires using fire hoses, but in (8) we picture them using a saw or a claw to cut the car. Finally, a core frame element of cut namely, the object that is cut (here the car) is backgrounded and not mentioned. All of this happens automatically due to our capacity for flexible, selective projection during blending; we do not even notice that much more than simple constructional combination is required. But even for such standard Construction Grammar examples, we need a more elaborate, flexible, and principled cognitive mechanism to explain the construct than simple 'combination.' 'Combination' is a word we ascribe to the output performance, but what is required is a theory of what processes might produce that output. The claim that construction combination has taken place does not constitute a theory of the process of creative combination.

In this Element, we argue that conceptual blending is the domain-general process that Construction Grammar so far lacks. Blending is the heart of creative combination, and a theory of creative combination is what CxG needs in order to count as a cognitive theory. In a nutshell, we propose that the way we form, combine, learn, and change constructions is the way we think.

This Element will next review alternative proposals in linguistics for the creative combination of linguistic units inter alia, 'merge' (Chomsky 1995, 2021; Adger 2003; Epstein et al. 2022; Chomsky et al. 2023), unification (Shieber 1986), constraint satisfaction (Müller 2023: 511–519), juxtaposition and superimposition (Dąbrowska & Lieven 2005), coverage (Goldberg 2019), and associative links (Diessel 2019; Schmid 2020). While all of these approaches have considerable empirical descriptive power, we will show that for virtually all phenomena across the lexicon-syntax cline, a more creative mental operation is required to fully explain how speakers combine constructions in the working memory – one that accounts for the selectivity of the process as well as for the resulting emergent meaning. As we will argue, conceptual blending is the cognitive mechanism that best accounts for all of these phenomena. Moreover, we will show that Cognitive Grammar (Langacker 2006, 2008), a theory closely aligned with the goals of Construction Grammar, already assumes that blending is at the heart of composition in grammar.

Thereafter, we will discuss blending as a general mental operation and then illustrate blending in operation over a range of kinds of constructions, from morphological to clausal to discursive. We will explore how multimodal communication, which involves speech, gesture, action, the manipulation of elements in the environment, and other aspects of human communicative performance, crucially requires conceptual blending as an operation for assembling multimodal constructs.

In essence, our proposal is that any cognitive linguistic theory, and Construction Grammar in particular, requires a theory of creative combination that does not postulate a domain-specific combinatory mechanism and we argue that the theory of conceptual blending satisfies that requirement. We label the resulting approach, which takes conceptual blending as the central cognitive process underlying all construction combination, 'Creative Construction Grammar.'

3 Candidate Theories of Creative Combination

Traditional words-and-rules approaches to language assume that the combination of words into sentences is achieved via syntactic rules. In such frameworks, words are the meaningful units of language, while syntactic rules are purely structural, combinatory operations. The latest and probably most prominent words-and-rules theory is Generative Grammar (Chomsky 1995, 2021; Chomsky et al. 2023). In stark contrast to cognitive linguistic theories, Generative Grammar holds that the main components of language are innate, domain-specific principles and parameters. To explain, for example, how words combine, this approach maintains that "the simplest combinatorial operation is binary set-formation, Merge in contemporary terminology" (Chomsky 2021: 13). Merge is a language-domain-specific operation that takes two words, such as *eat* and *pizza*, and combines them into an unordered set {*eat, pizza*} that still needs to be linearized via a language-specific parameter (yielding the sequence *eat pizza* in English and *Pizza essen* in German; for details see Chomsky et al. 2023).

Cognitive Linguistics can be seen as a rebuttal to Generative Grammar, criticizing the latter's reliance on language-specific and innate knowledge. Instead of postulating language-specific operations, cognitive linguists argue that a "parsimonious account of language would be in terms of cognitive abilities that humans are known to possess for reasons independent of language" (Enfield 2017: 13). In this vein, it would require substantial empirical support for cognitive linguists to postulate a language-specific process such as merge for the combination of words into sentences. Why should humans have ever evolved a language-specific set-forming computational operation that contains no information on linear order? From a Cognitive Linguistic perspective, we should instead look for a domain-general process to account for construction combination. Yet this immediately raises the question: Is there such a domain-general process that accounts for the combination of words?

An intuitive candidate might be 'combine.' Humans routinely combine physical objects (e.g., a stone and a wooden rod) into tools (a hammer) or mental concepts (such as 'breakfast' and 'lunch') into novel ideas ('brunch'). However, as these examples illustrate, neither of these processes is a case of simple combination. A hammer is not just a stone and a wooden rod, it is a single tool that has a functional use that goes beyond what one could do with the individual parts (i.e., it has an emergent function beyond its parts). Similarly, brunch is not just breakfast *and* lunch, it is a meal that is, among other things, prototypically scheduled between the latter two. In this Element, we want to take a closer look at the mental process that allows us to combine linguistic signs into larger units. In the cognitive linguistic spirit, our goal is to identify the domain-general cognitive operation that explains the (apparently) simple combination of *arm* and *chair* into *armchair* but also accounts for more creative combinations such as *brunch*. In the following, we will therefore start by surveying the combinatory mechanisms that have so far been proposed in the cognitive linguistic and constructionist literature, always asking whether these really count as domain-general cognitive processes and whether they provide a cognitively plausible explanation.

3.1 Formal CxG

3.1.1 Unification

Formal Construction Grammar approaches explicitly draw on processes from mathematical and computational sciences to model construction combination: Berkeley Construction Grammar, for example (see, e.g., Fillmore & Kay 1993, 1995; Fillmore 2013) used 'unification' (see, e.g., Shieber 1986; Müller 2023: 328–331) to combine constructions into constructs.

Unification grammars (Shieber 1986) include formal approaches such as Functional Unification Grammar, Definite-Clause Grammars, Lexical-Function Grammar, Generalized Phrase Structure Grammar, and Head-Driven Phrase Structure Grammar. Linguistic knowledge in these approaches is represented in attribute-value matrices (AVMs) such as CAT: N (for an attribute CATEGORY whose value is NOUN). The mathematical foundations of AVMs are so-called Directed Acyclic Graphs (DAGs), with the unification of two DAGs being defined by precise mathematical algorithms of graph theory (see Harary 1969). In (only slightly more) informal parlance, unification is a formal, algorithmic process "for solving sets of identity constraints" (Sag, Wasow & Bender 2003: 56, footnote 7; for a more technical definition, see Müller 2023: 329). For the sake of illustration, take the following, simplified example: the transitive verb *love* selects for a subject NP and an object NP (SUBCAT <NP, NP>). Upon being combined with an NP such as *football*, unification would identify the latter as an eligible object of the verb and unify the two into a VP *love football* that in a next step still requires a subject (SUBCAT <NP, *football*>). Berkeley Construction Grammar employed a definition of construction unification that led to various computational problems (see Müller 2023: 328–331; Sag, Boas, and Kay 2012: 6). But beyond Berkeley Construction Grammar, there are a great number of formal syntactic theories that have successfully implemented unification-based formalisms for the combination of words into phrases and sentences (inter alia, Generalized Phrase Structure Grammar [Gazdar, Klein, Pullum & Sag 1985], Head-driven Phrase Structure Grammar [Pollard & Sag 1994], or Lexical Functional Grammar [Bresnan & Kaplan 1982]). So we are not disputing that unification is a powerful computational process that allows for the successful formal modeling of linguistic competence. But is this how humans actually combine constructions in their minds? If this were in fact the case, then that would mean that Construction Grammar postulates a language-specific mechanism, namely unification, for the combination of constructions, something that Cognitive Linguistics tries to avoid at all costs. As far as we know, no one has ever claimed that unification is a domain-general cognitive process – and even if anyone made this claim, it demonstrably is not how humans combine thoughts (as will be discussed). As we will show, the cognitive linguistic arguments against unification are the same as those that can be levied against constraint satisfaction as the single mechanism of construction combination: These are purely additive operations with no room for selective projection or emergent meaning. Let us turn now to constraint satisfaction to illustrate these shortcomings of formal construction combination mechanisms.

3.1.2 Constraint Satisfaction

Instead of unification, more recent constructionist approaches such as Sign-based Construction Grammar (Boas & Sag 2012; Michaelis 2010, 2013), Fluid Construction Grammar (Steels 2011, 2013, van Trijp 2014), or Embodied Construction Grammar (Bergen & Chang 2005, 2013) use constraint satisfaction to model construction combination.[4] In these 'constraint-based' approaches, constructions are seen as constraints and a specific construct such as (8) will simply be checked as to whether it is licensed by appropriate constructions. Van Eecke & Beuls (2018: 344–348) impressively illustrate how a sentence like (8) is analyzed in such an approach, showcasing a Fluid Construction Grammar analysis. As they note, the Fluid Construction Grammar parser tries to freely combine all activated

---

[4] Sag, Wasow, & Bender (2003: 56, footnote 7) note that "[u]nification is an operation for merging descriptions of a certain form whose effect is equivalent to conjunction of constraints." See Müller (2008: 35, footnote 3) for more details on the differences between unification and constraint satisfaction. None of these issues, however, are material for the present discussion.

constructions, with "[c]onstructions [being] … activated in any order, as soon as the constraints in their conditional part are satisfied" (2018: 346). Thus, the definite NP construction matches and licenses the string *the man* in (8) and the Resultative construction matches and licenses the semantic and syntactic roles of *firefighters*, *the man*, and *free* (and so on). In contrast to generative approaches, which only consider structures to be grammatical if they are fully generated by the grammar, constraint-based approaches are more flexible and allow for partial matching of structures such as fragments as long as no constraints are violated (for a more detailed discussion of generative–enumerative vs. constraint-based approaches see Müller 2023: 511–519). Consequently, constraint-based approaches are highly successful at parsing natural language data. Again, however, we would like to ask whether this is an adequate model of the cognitive operations that underlie human language processing: Constraint-based analyses are in essence checking whether the output of construction combination is licensed by the constraints imposed by the existing constructions, but they cannot be said to drive or motivate construction combination. Let us illustrate this point with the following example:

(10) the more opaque that atmosphere is$_{C1}$
 the less conductive it is$_{C2}$
 the bigger the temperature difference you need to cross it.$_{C3}$
 (ICE-GB:S2A-043-F104; from Hoffmann 2017a: 5)

(10) is an instance of the Comparative Correlative construction, a constructional constraint that conventionally comprises two clauses (Culicover & Jackendoff 1999; Goldberg 2003: 220; Hoffmann 2017a; for a more detailed analysis of the construction see Hoffmann 2019b, 2022a: 230–231): a first clause (C1: *the more opaque that atmosphere is*) that is interpreted as the protasis/independent variable for a second clause that is seen as the apodosis/dependent variable (C2: *the less conductive it is*). Normally, the Comparative Correlative construction thus licenses bi-clausal constructs such as *the more opaque that atmosphere is*$_{C1}$, *the less conductive it is*$_{C2}$, with a meaning that can roughly be paraphrased as 'as the atmosphere becomes more opaque C1 → so it becomes less conductive C2.' In (10), however, the second clause is not only the apodosis to the preceding clause but also the protasis to a second Comparative Correlative construct (*the less conductive it is*$_{C2}$, *the bigger the temperature difference you need to cross it.*$_{C3}$). Now, complex constructs such as (10) receive a straightforward post-hoc explanation in constraint-based approaches: Both the first pair of sentences (C1 and C2) as well as the second pair (C2 and C3) match the Comparative Correlative construction and can be

licensed by it. Note, however, that this analysis is identical to the one that would be given had the speaker simply repeated the second clause, so that he would have uttered two Comparative Correlative constructs in direct succession as in (11):

(11) a. the more opaque that atmosphere is$_{C1}$
the less conductive it is$_{C2}$
b. the less conductive it is$_{C1}$
the bigger the temperature difference you need to cross it.$_{C2}$
(from Hoffmann 2017a: 5)

Again, we are not denying that constraint-based analyses are extremely successful at modeling examples such as (11). From a cognitive linguistic perspective, however, there is a crucial difference as to whether a speaker chooses (10) over (11). Instead of analyzing (10) in terms of constraint satisfaction, we argue that a cognitively more adequate account is to describe it in terms of conceptual blending. In (10), we have two instances of the Comparative Correlative construction that are blended into a single construct that, as part of its emergent meaning, expresses the correlative-causal relationship of the three clauses more tightly than (11). So, while constraint-based analyses might be able to assess the degree to which a construct matches the grammar of a language (in usage-based terms, its 'coverage' [Goldberg 2019]; discussed later), blending can explain how and why speakers create (10) and (11), and why they might prefer the former over the latter in certain contexts.

We want to argue that formal operations such as merge, unification, or constraint satisfaction are inadequate metaphors for the cognitive combination of constructions that Cognitive Linguistics and Construction Grammar want to model: First of all, none of these formal approaches are driven by semiotic considerations – algorithms drive these combinatorial processes, not meaningful intent. Consequently, while these operations provide in-depth post-hoc analyses, they do not provide an explanation for how and why speakers combine constructions in a particular way. Secondly, in the linguistic literature, these formal processes are either explicitly (merge) or implicitly (unification and constraint satisfaction) defined as domain-specific procedures. Third, as we will illustrate in more detail in Section 3.2, construction combination is never simply additive. It is selective, and it frequently gives rise to emergent meaning.

Formal, language-specific combination processes are, therefore, inadequate to model the cognitive combination of constructions. But what about usage-based approaches to CxG: Are the processes postulated by these accounts more convincing?

3.2 Usage-Based CxG

3.2.1 Juxtaposition and Superimposition

Within usage-based linguistics, Dąbrowska & Lieven (2005) directly propose a theory of creative composition of the sort needed in Construction Grammar. They argue that only two basic operations, juxtaposition and superimposition, are required. As they write,

> [t]he production of novel expressions involves the combination of symbolic units using two operations: juxtaposition and superimposition ... Juxtaposition involves linear composition of two units, one after another. Note that the two units can be combined in either order ... In superimposition, one unit (which we call the "filler") elaborates a schematically specified subpart of another unit (the "frame"). (Dąbrowska & Lieven 2005: 442–443)

In line with their usage-based approach, Dąbrowska & Lieven (2005: 441–444) assume that symbolic thinking (storing pairings of form and meaning, i.e., constructions) is central to humans. Moreover, they maintain that language acquisition is the learning of concrete and schematic constructions, and that constructions are combined via juxtaposition and superimposition. Dąbrowska & Lieven's analysis is a considerable improvement on (and empirically clearly superior to) postulating abstract and innate syntactic operations. At the same time, there are several issues that we would like to draw attention to. First of all, the way that juxtaposition and superimposition are defined marks them as domain-specific processes. It could, of course, be argued that juxtaposition is merely an additive procedure that can also be found outside of language. Superimposition, however, is specifically defined in a language-specific way (i.e., the phonological as well as semantic integration of a filler into the slot of a schematic construction; Dąbrowska & Lieven 2005: 444). As mentioned earlier, in line with the Cognitive Linguistic enterprise, we argue that such language-specific operations should be avoided at all cost, provided a domain-general process is readily available to explain the data. As we will show, blending is such a domain-general process, and the advantages of our Creative Construction Grammar approach will become particularly obvious when we discuss multimodal communication in Section 4.6 on Blending and Multimodality and Section 5.7 on Multimodal CxG.

What Dąbrowska & Lieven label 'juxtaposition' is called 'composition' in blending theory (Fauconnier & Turner 2002: 48). But in contrast to what blending theory calls 'composition,' Dąbrowska & Lieven's 'juxtaposition' is merely an additive procedure that combines two or more constructions without any interpretative component: "[l]inear juxtaposition signals that the meaning of the two expressions are to be integrated, but the construction itself does not spell out how this is to be done, so it must be inferred by the listener" (Dąbrowska & Lieven 2005: 442). Thus, while the domain-specific operation of juxtaposition requires an additional interpretative process, blending offers a domain-general analysis of composition that includes interpretation (as well as selective projection and emergent meaning, something that juxtaposition cannot account for). Similarly, what Dąbrowska & Lieven label 'superimposition' is known in blending theory as 'simplex blending' (Fauconnier & Turner 2002: 119). Again, in contrast to simplex blending, superimposition is only additive in nature and cannot account for emergent structures or selective projection, particularly in multimodal communication.

Dąbrowska & Lieven (2005) offer a convincing empirical analysis of the phenomena that children exhibit during language acquisition: the learning of constructions and their combination by putting them next to each other (juxtaposition) or combining them (superimposition). As they admit themselves, what is missing from this account is an explanation of how and why children do this. As we will show, conceptual blending not only accounts for these combination operations, but also offers a cognitive explanation for the cognitive semiotic processes that underlie and drive constructional combination.

3.2.2 Coverage

In her latest monograph, Goldberg (2019) explicitly addresses the creativity and partial productivity of constructions, focusing particularly on the latter phenomenon. A major innovation of her approach is the notion of coverage – the idea that the acceptability of a new construct is based on its similarity to the existing constructions that a speaker has previously entrenched. Goldberg proposes that instances of each construction cluster together in a hyper-dimensional space and that from this clustering generalizations emerge, which include information on semantics, information structure, syntax, and morphological and phonological constraints. As instances accumulate, new clusters can emerge, and these clusters are emergent constructions. Novel expressions are thus licensed by existing constructions to the extent that the existing combination of constructions covers the hyper-dimensional space required to include the novel expression. The principle of coverage is formalized using standard linear algebra modeling via vectorization:

> Clustering algorithms in Bayesian models do this by assigning each new utterance (each usage event) to an existing cluster that maximizes the fit between the new usage and the cluster, while taking into account the prior probability of each cluster.

Barak et al. (2014) have proposed such a model in which each usage event is represented by a vector of feature values (Fi), that includes a representation of the verb's semantics, the utterance's semantics, and the argument structure's syntactic properties ... The model learns incrementally just as human learners do. It assigns the very first usage event its own cluster; the next usage event is then assigned either to the existing cluster, if it is sufficiently similar to the previous usage event, or to a new cluster (the degree of dissimilarity that is tolerated is set by a parameter). (Goldberg 2019: 70)

The principle of coverage recognizes the need for developing and constraining a theory of constructional productivity. It offers a usage-based explanation of how speakers can extend their constructional repertoire, and as such, we think it has greatly furthered our understanding of the degree to which novel constructs are influenced and shaped by the existing constructional network. At the same time, coverage is clearly not intended to be a comprehensive theory of creative combination. The main focus of Goldberg is to account for "the partial productivity of grammatical constructions" (2019: 4), to explain "[h]ow native speakers know to avoid certain expressions while nonetheless using language in creative ways" (2019: 3). As a result, the main property of coverage is its inherently conservative nature: A novel construct is only licensed to the degree it matches a speaker's existing constructional knowledge. Constructions from this point of view are emergent clusters of form-meaning associations in a hyper-dimensional conceptual space. New expressions are then heard and are consequently associated with existing clusters. This, however, raises the question of how those new expressions, those new constructs, were formed in the first place, before hearers learned them in response to performances by others.

As a case in point take Perek's impressive (2016) study on the VERB *the hell out of* NP-construction (e.g., *Dudek said he'd once beaten the hell out of a Pepsi machine that took his money*. COCA[5] 2001 FIC SouthernRev). Perek found that the construction comprises several semantic subclusters which form the construction's coverage, such as psychverbs (e.g., *fascinate*, *please*, or *like*) or physical actions causing harm (e.g., *beat*, *knock*, or *slap*; 2016: 172–174). In line with the coverage hypothesis, he was able to further show that the productivity of these different clusters depended on their density, that is, the number of existing uses (Perek 2016: 174–179; see also Goldberg 2019: 67). Yet how did these clusters emerge in the first place? Any appeal to coverage, in essence, runs into the issue of regressus ad infinitum: When

---

[5] Corpus of American English (COCA): www.english-corpora.org/coca/ [last accessed 18 August 2025].

the construction was first coined, by definition, no cluster existed. Previous studies (Hoeksema & Napoli 2008) had postulated that the source construction was one found in the context of religious writings describing exorcism (*a priest beating the devil out of someone*), in which *the devil* was still interpreted as an affected object. Later, *the devil* was supposed to have been "'bleached' to the extent that it became solely an intensifier" (Hoeksema & Napoli 2008: 371). However, Hoeksema & Napoli (2008: 373) already mentioned a second potential source construction (e.g., *Mrs. Whaling would scare the life out of her with her tales of fearful adventure in the Indian country*; COHA 1884 FIC QueerStoriesBoys), in which the postverbal NP *the living daylights/lights* only had an adverbial meaning (i.e., it expressed that an event was particularly scary). Hoffmann & Trousdale (2022) then found that in the critical period of the nineteenth century, other potential input constructions existed that had a postverbal NP without referential meaning, merely expressing intensification (*She can knock the spots out of these boys at that game*. 1887, source Oxford English Dictionary, s.v. *spot*, meaning she soundly beat these boys or *They took the starch out of that Twelfth Maine, sir*; COHA 1867 FIC MissRavenelsConversion, meaning they soundly beat the Twelfth Maine). In addition to this, the NP *the devil* had been used as a non-referential expression of a speaker's heightened emotion since the eighteenth century (*What the Devil do you do without your Shoes!*; 1739, Old Bailey Corpus[6] 17390502_25). Hoffmann & Trousdale (2022) argued that several different routes might have led to the present-day construction VERB the N_{Taboo} out of construction (Hoffmann 2021): Some speakers might have drawn on the exorcism construction together with the eighteenth-century non-referential *the devil* construction. Others might have used the idiomatic *starch* and/or *spots* constructions together with the exorcism construction. Alternatively, many other combinations are possible (e.g., blending *the scare the life out of* construction and the eighteenth-century non-referential *the devil* construction as well as many other combinations). Hoffmann & Trousdale (2022) use this construction to show that multiple input constructions can allow different speakers to converge on the same novel construction. Whatever route speakers and hearers might have taken, all of these combinations require selective projection (of, e.g., *the devil* as a marker of heightened speaker emotion, postverbal NPs such as *the spots/the starch* as non-referential markers of intensification, the exorcism construction for the formal *the hell out of*

---

[6] Old Bailey Corpus (OBC): https://fedora.clarin-d.uni-saarland.de/oldbailey/ [last accessed 18 August 2025].

sequence, etc.) to get an emergent new blended construction (FORM: [[NP$_i$ V$_j$ [*the* N$_{TABOO}$ *out of*]$_k$ NP$_l$] ↔ MEANING: [SEM$_i$ excessively$_k$ PRED$_j$ SEM$_l$]]; adapted from Hoffmann & Trousdale 2022: 368).

What in a coverage approach accounts for the speaker's ability to make new constructs? What accounts for the original creation of the constructions in the history of language usage? What accounts for the original creation of constructions in the history of the species? What Goldberg proposes seems to be a system of inferring a construction, or a change in a construction, from encounters with its usage. This is a system for recognizing constructions that are in use or perhaps attributing grammaticality to utterances. It is a new proposal for a type of language acquisition process, which learns constructions from utterances that are built out of those very constructions, and as such, it is an important mental process in Construction Grammar. But it is neither a full theory of how those utterances come into being in the first place, nor is it a theory of how the speaker can combine constructions to create the construct that the learner ingests as new data (whether for the purposes of learning or for reinforcing a construction). Accordingly, we do not see how 'coverage' provides a complete theory of creative combination.

Creative language use, of course, always draws on the constructional networks available to speakers (being one of the five Cs in Hoffmann's [2024, 2025, fc.] 5C model of constructional creativity). However, limiting novel uses to more or less creative extensions of existing constructions fails to account for the selective nature of constructional combination as well as the novel emergent meanings that go beyond what the input constructions seem to offer. Creative (and, as we will argue, non-creative) language use requires an advanced blending operation of constructions in the working memory that is much more flexible and dynamic.

3.2.3 Combination in Dynamic Network Approaches: Association, Sequential Relations, and Co-semiosis

One cognitive linguistic model that explicitly focuses on the emergent and dynamic nature of language is Schmid's (2020; see also 2010) Entrenchment-and-Conventionalization (EC-) Model. The EC-Model is a usage-based model of language as a dynamic complex-adaptive system, continuously evolving through interactions between usage, conventionalization, and entrenchment: Language changes diachronically in virtue of feedback loops created by interactions; language accordingly responds fluidly to new communicative needs and contexts. The EC-Model emphasizes emergentist association: linguistic conventions and knowledge emerge from the repeated use of language in various contexts; associations between forms and meanings, as well as between different forms themselves, become stronger with repeated use, leading to the conventionalization and entrenchment of linguistic elements. 'Entrenchment' refers to the strengthening of cognitive representations of linguistic elements through repeated use, making these elements more easily and quickly activated in the mind. 'Conventionalization' involves the establishment and maintenance of linguistic norms within a speech community. Entrenchment and conventionalization are presented as interdependent and mutually reinforcing, driving the continual adaptation and evolution of language. The EC-Model also highlights the importance of interpersonal effort in the conventionalization process. Interpersonal activities, such as co-semiosis (mutual understanding during communication), co-adaptation, and co-construction, are crucial for the establishment of linguistic conventions. They require active participation and cooperation between speakers, and this cooperation undergirds the conventionalization of linguistic forms and structures.

There is much in the elaborate EC-Model to applaud, and we feel no need to oppose anything in the brief description of the EC-Model presented here. Crucially, though, the processes proposed in the EC-Model are not cognitive processes and are certainly not domain-general processes: Instead, entrenchment and conventionalization are outcomes of processes. Our contribution is to propose, and defend, the hypothesis that blending is the domain-general cognitive process that leads to outcomes such as entrenchment and conventionalization. Furthermore, entrenchment and conventionalization as discussed in the EC-Model do not address the central operations of creativity, selective projection, and emergent structure in both mental spaces and mental space networks, or any of the other aspects of meaning construction analyzed in conceptual integration theory. We agree wholeheartedly that interpersonal effort is crucial to language dynamics but ask what makes that interpersonal effort possible? What makes it possible to have an elaborate conception of other minds and their role in interactive discourse, including our conceptions of what they are trying to do, and our conceptions of their conceptions of what we are trying to do, and our conceptions of their conceptions of our conceptions of what they are trying to do, and so on? These layers of conceptions, of other minds, of their viewpoints and their intentions, of their complicated labor in communicative interaction, including their conceptions of us, and their conceptions of our conceptions of them, and so on, are indispensable to co-semiosis. Blending is the cognitive engine of such conceptions. Constructors and co-constructors interact in co-semiosis. Their conceptions of their minds and their efforts, indeed of their interactive minds and their interactive efforts, are products of blending. It may be that a dynamic network model such as the EC-Model simply assumes that the domain-general cognitive operation of blending, with all its complicated processes, is available to the speakers and that such a model presents itself as exploring the consequences of blending. If so, then we offer no fundamental opposition or critique.

A similar highly valuable line of research on cognitive, usage-based varieties of Construction Grammar has been pursued by Holger Diessel (e.g., Diessel 2019, 2023). Diessel's analysis revolves around the idea that constructions are organized within a network called the constructicon. He proposes a multidimensional network approach influenced by usage-based linguistics. By emphasizing the observable network of constructions and their associations, Diessel's model, in our view, implicitly relies on the intricate processes of blending without explicitly incorporating them into his model. (Though conceptual blending is at least briefly mentioned as "a general mechanism of language use and cognition" Diessel 2019: 101, 107) The model's strength lies in mapping the relationships and associations between constructions, but it does not fully explore the domain-general cognitive mechanisms that generate these relationships in the first place, and similarly does not address creativity, selective projection, or emergent structure in both mental spaces and mental space networks, or any of the other aspects of meaning construction analyzed in conceptual integration theory. It similarly takes for granted the cognitive operations that make possible conceptions of other minds and their work in co-construction during interaction and collaboration.

Fauconnier & Turner (2002, and citations therein) argued that to fully explain human language one must point to the cognitive abilities possessed by human beings but not available to other mammalian and especially primate species. In their account, rudimentary forms of blending have been available from at least the stage of early mammals, depending on which kinds of integration phenomena one prefers to count as blending. They observe that 'blending' is merely a label and that what matters scientifically is not a label but analyses of the workings of relevant processes. Where one draws the line in integration phenomena for ascribing the label 'blending' is merely a matter of preference. They emphasized the performances in which other species surpass humans: Human beings cannot fly, photosynthesize, smell as well as a dog, or see as well as an eagle. The genome of the Norwegian spruce tree is seven times as large as the human genome. Fauconnier & Turner (2002) proposed that human capacities lie on a cline of blending: while we may share this cline with many other species, human evolution produced a slight advance in blending abilities. They analyzed how, in reality, a small difference in causes can produce a very large difference in effects. Various species are impressively communicative (not only with each other, but also with human beings) yet there is a sharp difference between the communicative abilities of non-human species and those that are species-wide for human beings, and this difference is crucial for a comprehensive theory of human Construction Grammar. The original Fauconnier-Turner line of argument about the cognitive basis of human communicative performance has been pursued in other publications (e.g., Turner 2014). A usage-based theory of the origin and development of full human language that rests on only cognitive abilities shared with other species is missing its central and indispensable component. Luckily, we propose that the needed component already exists and can be directly embraced: Conceptual Blending.

3.2.4 Composition and Integration

Within cognitive and functional approaches to language, there are many analyses of processes of language that look much like blending. The most prominent and thorough of these theories is Cognitive Grammar (Langacker 2006). Langacker writes, for example, that "[o]ne constructional schema can be incorporated as a component of another" (Langacker 2006: 46). These many analyses include considerations of coercion when two units combine (Taylor 2002: 287), partial sanctioning of a unit, and extension and innovation during the combination of units (Langacker 2008: 215–255). A close attention to the varieties of symbolic combination was present in Cognitive Grammar from its earliest days. For example, in his landmark 1986 introduction to the field in *Cognitive Science*, Langacker wrote,

- "When a head combines with a modifier, for example, it is the profile of the head that prevails at the composite-structure level." (1986: 13)
- "Each sense of *ring* depicted in Figure 1, for example, combines with the phonological unit [ring] to constitute a symbolic unit." (1986: 18)
- "An auxiliary verb, either *have* or *be*, combines with the atemporal predication and contributes the requisite sequential scanning." (1986: 27)
- "A modifier is a conceptually dependent predication that combines with a head, whereas a complement is a conceptually autonomous predication that combines with a head." (1986: 34)
- "It should be apparent, however, that the same composite structure will result if the constituents combine in the opposite order, with *Alice* elaborating the schematic trajector of *likes*, and then *liver* the schematic

landmark of *Alice likes*. This alternative constituency is available for exploitation, with no effect on grammatical relations, whenever special factors motivate departure from the default-case arrangement." (1986: 35)

It may be that Langacker and other cognitive and functional linguists would agree (no doubt with some amount of clarification or objection, and only to a certain extent) that such analyses presuppose general cognitive mechanisms not specific to language and that indeed the chief one they presuppose is *blending*. In response to this suggestion, Langacker wrote (personal communication, cited in Turner 2020):

> I fully agree that CG [Cognitive Grammar] "analyses presuppose general cognitive mechanisms not specific to language and that indeed the chief one they presuppose is blending." I have long taken it for granted that conceptual and grammatical structures can be characterized in terms of mappings between mental spaces, and in particular, that 'composition' amounts to (bipolar) blending. This conforms to my traditional description that component structures are 'integrated' to form the composite whole. Perhaps because it is so evident, I have not made the connection to conceptual integration theory as explicit as I perhaps should have done. Here is one succinct statement: "In composition, component structures undergo conceptual integration to form a composite structure that is more than just the sum of its parts" (Langacker 2017, 118). Slightly more elaborate indications of the affinity are found in (Langacker 2009: 47) and (Langacker 2015: 135–136).

In this Element, we now want to make explicit the role of conceptual blending as the sole source of linguistic combination that has implicitly been presupposed in previous cognitive linguistic approaches, as acknowledged for Cognitive Grammar by Langacker. We want to emphasize again that we support attempts to create mathematical and computational models of the kinds of combination we see in the development of language (phylogenetically and ontogenetically), language change, the formation of constructions, and the formation of constructs out of constructions. But we propose that theories like 'merge' do not provide a theory of creative combination (and are not cognitive); that theories like 'coverage' are still far from a theory of creative combination (and are not yet cognitive, although they might develop in that direction); and that the most prominent and influential theory of language in the fields of cognitive and functional linguistics, namely Langacker's Cognitive Grammar, already assume blending as the central process of combination.

In the rest of this Element, we will briefly lay out principles of the mental operation of blending and analyze blending in action in language and communication.

4 Blending

Conceptual blending occurs when various input ideas, meanings, and conceptual structures, often starkly in conflict, are *selectively* combined into a conceptual structure not identical to any of the inputs, often with an emergent structure of its own.

Now, all cognitive models ultimately aim to be compatible with neurological models of the human mind (though see Hudson 2010: 71–72). As we mentioned in Section 1, the neurocognitive underpinnings of the processes of human cognition are not yet fully understood. A great number of mental processes, however, can successfully be modeled using network analyses (for an in-depth introduction, see Hills 2025). Conceptual blending also draws on network analyses, with many subprocesses being modeled by networks. Readers who are interested in the full details of these networks are referred to Fauconnier & Turner (2002) or Turner (2014). In the following, we will at least briefly mention the subnetworks that are relevant for our Creative Construction Grammar hypothesis.

Conceptual blending networks arise, as far as has been explored, across all conceptual domains. Work can be done at any spot in the network at any time: Indeed, many blending networks begin by taking a single mental space and assuming that it can be unpacked to establish two or more input spaces, so that the mental space becomes a blend through backward projection. Blends can be partially reconceived and redeveloped by reconceiving inputs under pressures of various kinds. There are many such patterns of operation over what comes to count as a blending network, once it is achieved. Blending is a process over conceptual structure, not a diagram. It can occur over mental space networks with any kind of structure. Mental spaces can have communicative constructions as part of their assembly. Blending can work on these constructions just as it can work on the rest of the elements in a mental space network.

A blend is a mental space in a conceptual network. The conceptual network may be highly dynamic and may contain many such mental spaces. The blend often helps us manage that conceptual network, including its construction and dynamism. For example, consider Bill and Peter, a pair of brothers-in-law, each happy. Bill is a mathematically-talented professor in the Eastern time zone who likes both investing and San Francisco. Peter is a stockbroker in San Francisco. Bill wonders, analogically: Should he move to San Francisco, be a stockbroker, and get a huge raise? No, he concludes upon reflection: If he were Peter, he would be miserable, because Bill is a night owl but Peter must rise at 5:30 a.m. Pacific Time to deal with the stock market's opening at 9:30 a.m. Eastern Time. Mentally,

Bill has created a new, blended person, Bill-as-Peter, who is miserable, even though misery is not in any of the inputs.

Blending is still a fairly new theory, first advanced in talks in 1993, with its initial publication in 1994 (Fauconnier & Turner 1994). It is a general theory of conceptual mapping and combination. It is not an alternative to prior, more specific theories but rather (at least in part) a generalization of them. It proposes to build on narrower predecessor theories by generalizing their achievements, uniting various theories of more limited application. The founders and practitioners of blending theory claim that it improves those theories by accounting for phenomena in their wheelhouses that have previously proved to be intractable or which were ungeneralized within the previous specific theories.

Blending has been deployed since 1993 to make sense of human behavior across all domains of higher-order human cognition – mathematical invention, scientific discovery, reasoning, inference, categorization, art, music, dance, social cognition, advanced tool innovation, religion, and so on – which is to say, across very many domains other than *grammar* (for an overview and list of relevant publications, see http://blending.stanford.edu). It is therefore a natural next step to ask whether this powerful domain-general process is not also the mechanism that humans draw on to combine constructions.

The now-vast body of research on blending focuses on blending as a basic mental operation, whose rudiments seem to be available across many species, but whose advanced form belongs only to human beings. Human beings are on a cline with other species in respect to this mental ability, but a small difference in causes can sometimes produce relatively huge, all-important differences in effects, and this, blending theory proposes, is a central part of any account of why human beings are so creative as a species. Here, we are concerned with the ways in which advanced blending makes advanced communication possible. Evolution has built in a few basic form-meaning pairs (e.g., a mental conception arises when a large scary animal growls at us); simple conditioning seems to be able to construct some other form-meaning pairs through associative mechanisms and conditioning (in experiments, even a pigeon can learn that pressing the red button delivers the food). But the human ability to form large relational networks of form-meaning pairs and to combine them into performances depends upon a level of quick creativity unevidenced in any other species. In other words, human language depends upon this level of creative connection and combination. That is, it depends upon the basic mental operation of blending, and in particular, upon its advanced, human-level modes of operation.

4.1 Requirements for a Theory of Construction Grammar, and How Blending Meets Them

Theory typically proceeds by taking a domain of phenomena and attempting to build a model whose operation matches those phenomena, within some tolerance, and correcting the model when confronted with disconfirming phenomena. It is based on the understanding that, to avoid circularity, the improved model must be tested against out-of-sample data (that is, data that did not influence the construction of the model). This is the basic process of scientific generalization: hypotheses prompted by one set of data are tested to see whether they apply to data not involved in the making of hypotheses.

There are fundamental requirements for any theory of Construction Grammar, and we claim blending meets them. We do not know of an alternative proposal that meets these requirements.

4.2 Requirement: Cognitive Theory

In the successful sciences, modeling a domain of phenomena does not proceed by ignoring relevant domains. Organic chemistry does not ignore inorganic chemistry. Cellular biology does not ignore physics. And all science abides by arithmetic.

Cognitive Linguistics must conform to this general scientific principle for cognitive dependencies that make advanced communication possible. In addition, cognitive linguists must face the fact that full human language, a very recent phenomenon evolutionarily, was presumably built from basic mental operations that are not language-specific.

Accordingly, a cognitive theory of Construction Grammar is obliged to show that the processes presupposed or asserted by the theory exist in human cognition generally, independent of language, or to include in the theory that the processes are language-specific and argue how they could have arisen to be so. To be sure, it can be alleged that language capacities that were established from preexisting capacities enjoyed some genetic uptake over the last fifty or one hundred thousand years (see, e.g., Everaert et al. 2017; Yang et al. 2017), but even that is methodologically not the very first resort if one prefers a cognitive theory. The Construction Grammarian is precluded from proposing that an operation is involved in 'combining constructions' unless it is a known operation of advanced human cognition. The mental operations of meaning construction are involved in language but are not necessarily specific to language. The Construction Grammarian may be prompted to hypothesize a process of combination in order to account for grammatical phenomena but has a prior commitment to do so only if that operation can be shown to operate outside of language, or to account for its arising solely within language.

We emphasize the fundamental distinction between a theory of human communication and a tool for researching grammatical data. The authors of this Element are proponents of the use of tools for researching grammatical data, as principals of Red Hen Lab (www.redhenlab.org), a big data science collaborative for the development of computational, AI, statistical, and technical instruments for tagging vast ecologically valid communicative data. One goal of Red Hen is to provide a data-testing ground for theories of communication. Red Hen deploys every computational system and tagging system it has time to manage and warmly welcomes all competing systems. Red Hen was, as far as we know, until very recently the only project in the world to tag big datasets (the current dataset has over 6 billion words) for the conceptual frames they involve, based on FrameNet 1.7 (Steen et al. 2018). The Red Hen tagging system is based on Linux, Python, and various machine-learning packages. But such computational tools are not meant to be models of human cognition or human language. They are instead tools for human beings who wish to search, recognize, and gather data, mostly to test hypotheses against those data. Research tools are designed for the task at hand. We place in the category of such research tools Head-Driven Phrase Structure Grammar, Generalized Phrase Structure Grammar, the computational aspects of Sign-Based Construction Grammar, and, originally, the various presentations of unification proposed in the several unpublished versions of the original Fillmore & Kay textbook on Construction Grammar (1993). These proposals for unification intend to produce all and only those constructs in an approved set of constructs, and this is a useful thing to do if the purpose is to tag language so that it can be searched for metadata (such as grammar; see Section 3.1). Again, this tool-building approach is not a theory modeling human cognition. Developing coding and computational procedures limited to this or that set of grammatical constructions is not cognitive theory.

Blending theory, by contrast, is a fully cognitive theory, demonstrating the operation of blending processes in every domain of cognition researchers have had time since 1993 to explore. Independent of debates in linguistics, researchers must acknowledge the fundamental and constant operation of blending processes in advanced human cognition. It is, we imagine, incontestable that such processes are available for grammar. It is by no means the case that a researcher must accept all the analyses blending theory has offered (e.g., its constitutive principles, governing constraints, or common patterns of compression of Vital Relations, such as mirror networks, representation networks, and Analogy-Disanalogy-to-Change-for-an-Identity Networks). Blending theory is embryonic, however powerful it may be: In its mere 30 years of existence, it has undergone sustained improvement.

Thirty years is a very short lifetime for a general theory of mapping and conceptual meaning. The special-case mapping theories that blending theory generalizes have Greek names because they have been the subject of study for millennia: category, metonymy, analogy, metaphor, climax, and a range of what the Greeks called *schemas* and the Romans called *figures*. As Gibbs (2017: 262) comments, "The astonishing idea that metaphor may be a basic scheme of human thought has been proposed by several scholars over the centuries." The assertion that the mapping systems called schemas or figures are conceptual is ancient. In classical antiquity, a writer like Demetrius (1995 [1932]) – essentially a reporter rather than an innovator – felt comfortable explaining in his work *On Style* that metaphoric conceptions can be as 'true' as any others, that the conceptual metaphoric mappings we see manifested in language are asymmetric, that everyday language is widely and ineradicably metaphoric, and that we understand linguistic constructions (to an extent) in terms of what we might now call figural projections of image-schemas. In Longinus's *On the Sublime* (1995 [1932]), we find the claim that figural understanding is all the more powerful when it is so automatic that we do not recognize its figural nature. Aristotle's detailed investigation of figurative language obscured, for some, his recognition of its conceptual role, but it was Aristotle who gave Edmund Burke the all-important verb – "to do metaphor well is to *see* (consider)" connections. When Aristotle defines metaphor as the transfer of a noun from one thing to another, he means transfer motivated by conceptual relations – either of category (genus to species, species to genus, species to species) or of analogy. Conceptual connection drives linguistic figuration: "To scatter seed is to sow, but there is no word for the action of the sun in scattering its fire. Yet this has to the sunshine the same relation as sowing has to the seed, and so you have the phrase 'sowing the god-created fire'" (Poetics XXI, 14; Aristotle 1995). Several literary critics have proposed that the everyday mind is irreducibly imaginative, or figurative. In 1936, I. A. Richards wrote that, "Fundamentally [metaphor] is a borrowing between and intercourse of thoughts ... Thought is metaphoric ... and the metaphors of language derive therefrom," (Richards 1936: 94) and C. S. Lewis wrote that understanding one story figurally in terms of another story belongs not principally to expression and not exclusively to literature, but rather, to *mind* in general, as a basic cognitive instrument (Lewis 1936: 44).

These theories are millennia-old. In contrast, blending theory is almost brand new, partially explaining its English name. Blending theory generalizes preceding theories. Further improvement of blending theory is inevitable and welcome; such improvement is natural for any new scientific theory. But unlike nearly all proposals for unification and constraint satisfaction in Construction Grammar approaches, the theory of blending is anything but ad hoc, arbitrary, modular, or restricted to communication. It is constrained by not only grammatical data but also all data relevant to the construction of meaning and conceptual networks. No one imagines that a special-focus theory – of category, metonymy, analogy, metaphor, climax, and so on – could provide a theory of unification and constraint satisfaction for Construction Grammar. But *blending* does. As far as we know, there is no other general theory of construction combination that is available for this job (see Section 3) – there is no rival hypothesis.

4.3 Requirement: The Development of Grammar in the Species

By all accounts, full human language is, phylogenetically, an extremely recent development. A researcher is free to hypothesize that language arose as a genetically instructed module operating according to language-specific mental operations and uninfluenced by preceding basic mental operations (Everaert et al. 2017; Yang et al. 2017). To the many scientific attacks on this hypothesis (e.g., Turner 1996, chapter 7, "Language"; Tomasello 2003), we here would only note the recent discovery that FOXP2 (a regulatory gene on chromosome 7 broadly active, including in brain development) has not changed in recent evolutionary history (Atkinson et al. 2018). Thus, while at one point researchers speculated that human specific mutations on FOXP2 enabled the development of language (Enard et al. 2002), Atkinson et al. (2018) were able to show that there is no evidence for the claim that the gene shows human-specific positive selection. In contrast to domain-specific approaches, and in line with Cognitive Linguistics, we take the view that for Construction Grammar to be a cognitive theory, it must at least make every attempt to ground the processes that it assumes for language in preceding mental operations that are known to operate robustly outside of language. Crucially, we believe that human language evolved due to a domain-general cognitive innovation – conceptual blending, which led to the association and compression of symbolic form-meaning pairings into constructions (thus spawning advanced symbolic thinking; Deacon 1997; Tomasello 1999), and, in a next step, enabling the creative combination of the constructions.

Evolution is a tinker: Innovation comes from the work of existing processes on existing material (Jacob 1977). To the extent that linguistic processes cannot be grounded in processes that are not language-specific, then we may, as a last resort, be driven to hypothesize the evolution of language-specific mechanisms, or at least the evolution of genetic support that made it easier to leverage existing processes to serve language.

As has been argued in Turner (1996) and Fauconnier & Turner (2002, 2008a, 2008b), blending provides a theoretical grounding for construction combination in Construction Grammar. We know of no elaborated rival to the blending hypothesis that does not depend upon stipulating arbitrary language-specific operations to make the model work, typically by adjusting those stipulations on the fly to fit the model to the target data. That is an excellent procedure for the construction of a Natural Language Processing tool to create metadata for an interactive system useful to human beings, but on principle it foregoes the ambition of creating a cognitive theory. The stipulation made for the model might accidentally, or intuitively, hit upon a process that is cognitive, but it would require a demonstration of the robust operation of that process across human cognition to make the stipulation satisfying as a cognitive theory.

Blending usually works on inputs that already exist to form a compressed blend in the network. It can involve any number of input spaces – work can be done at any place in the network at any time. It is also common that during blending inputs are rebuilt under the influence of backward projection from the blend. A basic form–meaning pair takes a form and a meaning in the ground and compresses them to create a construction, such as a lexical construction. The construction does not eliminate its inputs, and the user is not deluded: We all know of cases in which a speaker knows the meaning and can make the sound, but – we might say, colloquially – is *misusing* the word. That is, the speaker has the form and the meaning but not the expected form–meaning compression. For example, the visitor from Kansas might ask as we sail on the Pacific Ocean when we will return "back to the coast." The speaker is unconfused and has used forms that prompt for an exact meaning, but we still might say, "you mean 'back *ashore*'," because, for us but not the speaker, the *coast* is what you are headed to if you are driving from Kansas, but the *shore* is what you are headed to if you are sailing in from the Pacific Ocean. We, from the viewpoint of land, would call it 'the West Coast,' not 'the West Shore.' Others might have slightly different constructions. Part of understanding is to accommodate the usage of others, that is, to guess that their performance results from a blend (combination), one of whose inputs does not quite match ours but which we can imagine: this imagining of an input we did not previously have is highly creative. Accommodation itself (like learning, inventing, combining, etc.) requires a theory of creative blending.

Many mammals appear to have rudimentary capacities for blending, and, accordingly, rudimentary capacities for form-meaning pairing, but it is advanced blending operations that make full language possible. As Fauconnier & Turner (2002, chapter 9, "The Origin of Language") remark,

> [T]he world of human meaning is incomparably richer than language forms. Although language has been said to make an infinite number of forms available, it is a lesser infinity than the infinity of situations offered by the very rich physical mental world that we live in. To see that, take any form, such as "My cow is brown," and try to imagine all the possible people, cows, and shades of brown to which it might apply, as well as all the different uses of the phrase as ironic or categorical or metaphoric, including its use as an example in this paragraph. A word like "food" or "there" must apply very widely if it is to do its job. (Fauconnier & Turner 2002: 178)

The structure of a language is *small* relative to conceptual structure, connection, and innovation. Despite the limits on linguistic structure, language has the amazing ability to be put to use in any situation. The constructions commanded by any communicator will not include all those available in the language, but this does not doom the communicator to fail: The communicator can press into service some known constructions to communicate. We refer to this ability of subsets of constructions to be good enough for the task at hand as the 'equipotentiality' of language. For any situation, real or imaginary, there is always a way to use language to express thoughts about that situation. The key to this linguistic equipotentiality is blending.

Consider an example: Someone sees a termite doing something to wood. The meaning attached to the form 'food' certainly does not include wood, but people can make a blend of a person eating food and what the termite is doing to the wood. This blend is not an algorithmic unification of these two quite different input spaces but instead a new mental space constructed through selective projection from these inputs and conceptual elaboration to produce an emergent structure in the blend. Crucially, forms that apply to any of the input spaces (and there can be many) can be projected to the blend to pick out corresponding meaning there, despite its not conforming to the meaning in the input from

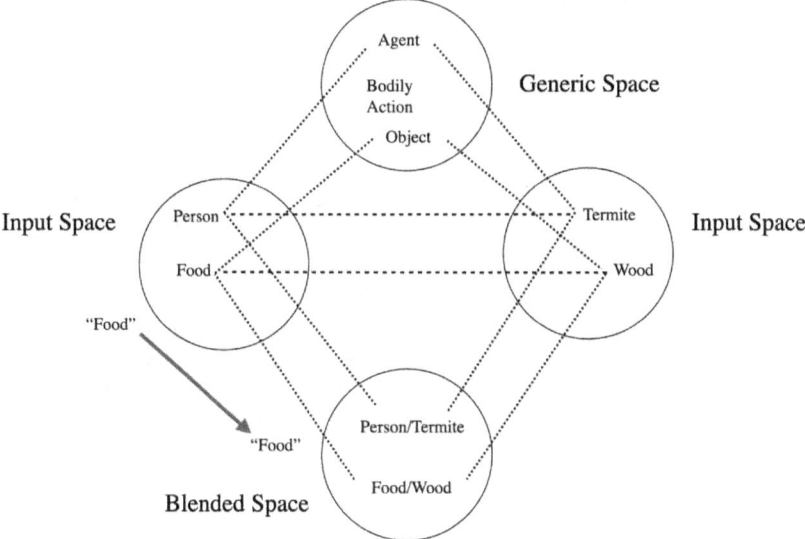

Figure 4 Termite Food

which it was projected. The wood can now be referred to as 'food.' This is an example of how blending solves the challenge of equipotentiality. Figure 4 sketches this process, but we hasten to repeat that the diagram is only for purposes of suggestion and presentation: Mental spaces are not actually in different physical or neurobiological spaces; the theory says nothing about circles and lines; and blending networks usually have many more than four mental spaces. Hence, the figure is just a visual suggestion of a dynamic and complicated process.

Such selective projection of constructions onto blends can also be illustrated using argument structure constructions. Take, again, the Resultative construction, whose template can schematically be given as FORM: [SBJ$_1$ V$_4$ OBJ$_2$ OBL$_3$] ↔ MEANING: 'A$_1$ causes B$_2$ to become C$_3$ by V$_4$-ing' (see Section 2). As Fauconnier & Turner (2002: 178–179) mention, this construction licenses a wide range of constructs (12–17) whose specific meanings actually differ in nontrivial ways from each other:

(12) She kissed him unconscious.

(13) Last night's meal made me sick.

(14) He hammered it flat.

(15) I boiled the pan dry.

(16) The earthquake shook the building apart.

(17) Roman imperialism made Latin universal.

As Fauconnier & Turner (2002: 178–179) note, in (12–17) the abstract Resultative construction is used to describe events that actually range over a vast expanse of actions and results:

> We find it obvious that the meaning of the resultative construction could apply to all these different domains, but applying it thus requires complex cognitive operations. The events described here are in completely different domains (Roman imperialism versus blacksmithing) and have strikingly different time spans (the era in which a language rises versus a few seconds of earthquake), different spatial environments (most of Europe versus the stovetop), different degrees of intentionality (Roman imperialism versus a forgetful cook versus an earthquake), and very different kinds of connection between cause and effect (the hammer blow causes the immediate flatness of the object, but eating the meal at one time causes sickness at a later time through a long chain of biological events).

Beyond the simplistic meaning pole given above ('A_1 causes B_2 to become C_3 by V_4-ing'), the abstract constructional template thus prompts for a complex conceptual integration in the working memory that compresses over Identity, Time, Space, Change, Cause-Effect, and Intentionality (see Fauconnier & Turner 2002: 178–179).

When Fauconnier & Turner made the first public presentation of blending (in a 1993 workshop with an audience including Ronald Langacker, George Lakoff, Seana Coulson, and many others), they explicitly cited Langacker's work on the cognitive creation of grammatical elements such as Noun and Verb as an implicit blending analysis. They explicitly presented conceptual metaphors as instances where a blending process had resulted in stable mappings often reflected in constructions, but they emphasized that those entrenched mappings could be awakened into a fuller blending network that provided new work and new emergent meanings. Blending theory does not reject preceding mapping theories but generalizes them. To be sure, it often proposes improvements in those mapping theories and proposes new generalizations across specific mapping theories, but in doing so it has always represented itself as building on and advancing them. Indeed, the essence of Construction Grammar – its view that knowing a language consists in knowing (and changing) a relational network of form–meaning pairs that blend to make expressions – has deep continuity with theories of language that have been in place since at least classical antiquity (see Turner 1998 for a review).

Because of language's power of equipotentiality through blending, accomplished speakers of an established language rarely need new constructions to express a new meaning. But still, Construction Grammar must include a cognitive theory of the origin of new constructions: New constructions have often been invented in recent history and they continue to be invented now. Fauconnier & Turner (2002) offer examples of the emergence of new constructions. The construction 'nominal compound' arises by taking two connected mental spaces, each with a form (noun) attached, and blending the input spaces while blending the two nouns into another noun, namely a noun phrase, Noun+Noun, as in *land yacht, girl scout, ballet school,* or *lace curtain*. One can further blend nominal compounds that are attached to meanings: *ballet school girl scout*. And so on. 'Y-*of*' constructions can be blended in many ways: *Ann is the boss of the daughter of Max* and *Prayer is the echo of the darkness of the soul* have the same structure as blending networks but quite different meanings and quite different lexical constructions. (For conceptual blending analyses of a great number of other syntactic examples see Fauconnier & Turner 1996; Hampe & Schönefeld 2003; and Turner 2018.)

Again, blending theory routinely cites preexisting theories as offering analyses that it in turn generalizes and expands. In a paper entitled "Blending as a Central Process of Grammar," Fauconnier & Turner (1996) write:

> It is apparent that the causative forms are superficially similar to basic transitive and ditransitive forms in the language. As Kemmer and Verhagen (1994) have pointed out, this is no accident: "Analytic causative constructions can best be described as extensions of simpler kinds of expressions, rather than as reductions from more complex underlying structures." Kemmer and Verhagen argue that there are cognitive models of causation based on force dynamics and interactions between participants, and that these models relate to basic models, including transitive and ditransitive event structures. We think this view is exactly right, and that Blending is the cognitive operation which allows the basic models to serve as inputs to the conceptual integration of more elaborate causal sequences. (In the same general spirit, Shibatani [1994] offers an insightful integrational account of possessor raising and ethical datives.)

Fillmore & Atkins (1992) analyze 'derived syntax,' which Turner (2008) calls 'blended syntax.' Fillmore & Atkins analyze *load with* as in *load the truck with hay* and *smear with* as in *smear the wall with mud* as syntactic blends that prompt for meaning blends (*load hay on the truck* and *fill the truck with hay* are available patterns for building *load the truck with hay* to prompt for a meaning in which the hay fills the truck completely; *smear mud on the wall* and *cover the wall with mud* are available patterns for building *smear the wall with mud* to prompt for a meaning in which the mud covers the wall completely). Frames of choice, possibility, and harm can be blended, and linguistic patterns available for expressing them – the main verb *risk* and the verbal constructions *wager on, invest in*, and *expose to* – can be blended at the formal level: *risk your money on a horse*; *risk your money in the stock market*; *risk your boat to the waves*. (See Turner [2015, 2018] for other cases of blending that produce new constructions.)

What were the non-language-specific basic mental operations that made it possible for human beings, as a species, to invent constructions, to use those constructions with equipotentiality, to invent new constructions, to 'unify' constructions into constructs, and to understand constructs as 'unifications' of constructions? This is a fundamental question that Construction Grammar must answer if it is to count as a cognitive theory of language. Our hypothesis is that advanced blending is the answer.

4.4 Requirement: The Development of Grammar in the Individual

An individual must from birth develop new constructions (including constructions that are new to the individual but not to the community), use constructions with equipotentiality, invent new constructions when needed, combine constructions into constructs, and understand constructs as combinations of constructions. What are the robust non-language-specific basic mental operations that make it possible for the individual human being to do so? As recent research has shown (for an overview see Tomasello 2014), humans coordinate and communicate with each other in ways that cannot be observed in any other species. Other great apes also exhibit complex social interaction, but a closer analysis of their behavior reveals that their motivation is ultimately always driven by their personal gains. In contrast to this, even three- or four-year-old children already cooperate with peers in a collaborative way that is not just driven by their own advantage. From an evolutionary perspective, humans thus seem to have evolved as an 'ultra-social animal' (Tomasello 2014): Mutual interdependence for survival gave rise to the cognitive ability of shared intentionality, the idea of acting on and understanding the world "as a kind of plural subject" (Tomasello 2014: 193).

Even before linguistic communication emerged, humans evolved two types of cognitive abilities that allowed them to share intentions and that proved vital for the emergence of language (Tomasello 2003): intention-reading and pattern-finding.

Intention-reading means that we as humans are predisposed to understand that other people do not necessarily think like us and that different people might have different intentions. However, a crucial prerequisite for this theory of mind is that advanced conceptual blending allows us to construct the mental states others might be in (Turner 2014: 31–63). Now, an important step that helps us guess what another person's intentions might be is to establish joint attention (by pointing at something or looking in the same direction). If we know what another person is focusing on at a specific moment in time, it becomes (slightly) easier to guess what they are thinking. Joint attention is thus an important first step in establishing someone else's intention – and it is also the first important step that every child must take when acquiring their first language (cf. Clark 2009: 27–32). Cognitively, joint attention is of course nothing but the process of blending our viewpoint with that of our interlocutor, something only made possible by our ability for conceptual blending (traces of which can be found in other species as well). Note the considerable positive ontogenetic as well as phylogenetic effect that advanced conceptual blending has. It is well known that human individuals differ considerably with respect to their personality traits (such as openness, extraversion, agreeableness, conscientiousness, and neuroticism; see, e.g., Nettle 2007). From a phylogenetic perspective, however, there are situations requiring behavior that is more cautious and other situations in which it is more important to throw all caution aside and simply act against a potential threat. Individuals cannot easily change a personality trait like neuroticism. But advanced conceptual blending allows groups of more or less cautious individuals to coordinate and negotiate the best solution for any problem. There is no doubt that humans do not always succeed in this, but compared to other species, advanced conceptual blending gives us a considerable evolutionary head start.

Pattern-finding is the second domain-general process that enables language learning. From a very early age onwards, humans are really good at detecting patterns. Even three- to four- month-old babies, for example, already notice that different types of cats typically look more similar to each other than to dogs (Rakison and Lawson 2013: 599–602), and when babies have been familiarized with cats only, they will spend more time looking at a new dog than at a new cat. Since babies focus longer on new objects than on ones that they are already familiar with, this shows us that even these small children have probably already formed a mental category for cats based on the similarities of all the cats that they have encountered. While a new cat can quickly be identified as an instance of this mental category, a new dog does not match the previous experience as well and therefore is more interesting and receives more attention.

In first-language acquisition, intention-reading and pattern-finding crucially interact: As Tomasello (2003) notes, language acquisition studies (e.g., Diessel & Tomasello 2000; Diessel 2006; Lieven et al. 2003; for an overview Diessel 2013, 2015) show that children first (around the age of 14 months) use short constructions such as *Bike!* or *More!*. This stage is sometimes called the 'one-word-stage', but this term is actually a bit misleading. Children do not just utter simple word constructions (in which a phonetic form such as [baɪk] is paired with the context-independent, i.e., semantic meaning of 'bicycle'). Instead, they use these linguistic symbols to express their intentions with respect to a specific situation (see Tomasello 2006: 23). When a child says *Bike!*, it might mean that the child wants to ride a specific bike. By uttering *More!*, the child maybe wants to "request or describe the recurrence of objects or events" (Tomasello 2006). While the precise meaning of these uses might be child-specific, the prime function of these first constructions (which are also known as 'holophrases') is generally pragmatic: They are an expression of the children's intention, addressed to a specific hearer in a given communicative situation. In essence, what children do is to exploit the equipotentiality of language and their parents' ability for intention-reading: Into their short linguistic constructs they blend and compress complex pragmatic meanings and they rely on their interlocutors' skill of advanced conceptual blending to unpack these meanings and their intentions. As we argue, the social and pragmatic meanings being modeled are not additional inferences that are performed after processing an abstract level of semantic content (as implied by approaches such as Relevance Theory; Sperber & Wilson 1995). Due to their ultra-social nature (Tomasello 2014), humans always blend social and pragmatic inputs into their linguistic blends.

Conceptual blending is thus an integral process that is heavily employed during the use and acquisition of children's first linguistic constructions. And it remains the central mechanism for construction combination thereafter: After their holophrase stage, between the ages of 18 and 20 months, children proceed to so-called 'item-based constructions' (also known as 'pivot schemas/pivot words' [see also Diessel 2013, 2015]). (18), for example, gives typical item-based constructs uttered by a child (Braine 1963):

(18) Constructs licensed by the *More X* construction
(Braine 1963; cited in Braine 1976: 7)
a. more car (meaning: 'I want to drive around some more')
b. more cookie (meaning: 'I want another cookie')
c. more hot (meaning: 'I want another hot thing')
d. more read (meaning: 'I want you to keep reading')
e. more sing (meaning: 'I want you to keep singing')

The *More X* construction that the child seems to have entrenched is partly fixed and partly schematic (FORM: [mɔː] X) and has a meaning that can roughly be paraphrased as MEANING: 'I want X to reoccur' (Hoffmann 2022a: 22). It is the first step towards abstract argument structure constructions, which children acquire slightly later. Yet again, we would like to point out that item-based constructions are prompts that can only be understood by hearers drawing on advanced conceptual blending. Whether (18a) means that the child wants to be driven round once more or to be given another toy car can only be understood by the caretaker that is present when the construct is uttered. Similarly (18e) could mean that the child wants to sing more or that they want someone else to continue singing. In most situations, however, caretakers have no problem interpreting these constructs correctly, since they can draw on advanced conceptual blending to establish joint attention and to unpack the child's constructs. Caretakers unpack blends such as *more car* using input spaces such as linguistic prompts (the *More X* construction and the lexical construction *car*) as well as social and interpersonal information (such as what object could be identified as a car in the current joint attention frame and what their child enjoys doing with this object).

The same phenomena can also be observed during pidginization (see, e.g., Lefebvre 2004: 7–23; Velupillai 2015), that is, when two groups of speakers that share no common language or lingua franca come into limited contact and consequently 'invent a new language'. Since pidgins tend to have only a limited number of vocabulary items, they are said to use 'circumlocution' (i.e., paraphrases) to express more complex concepts that in other varieties of English are expressed by single words (Mesthrie et al. 2000: 290–291). Take the following examples from Tok Pisin:

(19) a. gras bilong fes 'beard (lit. grass belong face)'
b. gras bilong hed 'hair (lit. grass belong head)'
c. gras bilong ai 'eyebrow (lit. grass belong eye)'
d. wara bilong skin 'sweat (lit. water belong skin)'
(from Mesthrie et al. 2000: 291)

The item-based construction licensing the constructs in (19) has the FORM pole [X *belong* Y]. Semantically, it is a prompt for conceptually blending the element X from a domain of physical experience (here, grass and water) with another physical domain (here, body parts; see also Hoffmann 2022a: 245). What this example illustrates is that even in situations where people have to invent constructions to express a meaning for which they have no lexical resources yet, the equipotentiality of language together with the ability of advanced conceptual blending enables speakers to communicate easily and effectively.

There is, therefore, strong empirical evidence from ontogenetic language acquisition as well as from phylogenetic language evolution that advanced conceptual blending is key to combining constructions and expressing complex meanings. As far as we can see, there is no need to postulate any additional language-specific combinatory mechanism to explain how constructions are combined in the minds of speakers.

4.5 Requirement: Managing Creativity and Collective Action

As Engel (2005) argues, human beings are by nature highly flexible and variable, so much so that cultures must invent institutions to generate some predictability in human performance if we are ever to interact beneficially. Put differently, cultures invent institutions for the purpose of creating sufficient regularity and predictability to make collective action possible. In the last fifty thousand years or so – an eye-blink in evolutionary time – cultures have invented contracts, classrooms, courts, constitutions, retail counters, certified public accountants, and conjugal arrangements, among many other things. It is impossible to model collective action unconstrained by cultural institutions. Turner & McCubbins (2018) and McCubbins, McCubbins, & Turner (2021) have analyzed various cultural frames (e.g., the restaurant) for their role in providing such constraint.

Blending, although highly systematic and constrained, provides human beings with much greater creativity and unpredictability than could ever be workable for collective action, including communication. Collective action needs regularity and predictability; contracts, classrooms, courts, constitutions, and so on likewise need such regularity and predictability. Just so for constructions. Human beings can invent on the fly any number of form-meaning pairs, as we see in private communication between close participants who have a vast overlap in their understanding of the ground they inhabit, expect that all other participants share that overlap, and expect as well that these participants know all of this at any level of metaknowledge.

For efficient and reliable collective communication, culture strongly regulates the relational network of form-meaning pairs available to participants and thereby generates sufficient predictability to create the possibility of full human language. Whatever form-meaning blends and blends of form-meaning blends someone puts forward are immediately controlled by the constraint of uptake by the community, and that uptake is reduced to a trickle of what it could otherwise be by the fact that cultures teach the accepted network of form-meaning pairs and how they blend (a phenomenon Schmid 2020 captures by the term 'conventionalization'). Culture gates the degree and rate of change of such a collective network. For example,

1. Postclausal, retrogressive negation. From the 1970s through the 1990s, American speakers at least were exposed to the popularity of the postclausal *not*, as in: *I like your sweater. Not.* There were intonational aspects of this construction. There were precedents to build upon, such as *I like this not*. The postclausal *not* could have been picked up generally as a completely unmarked construction. But a half-century later, it remains a rare, marked, special-purpose construction. A speaker can invent such constructions, but culture gates them (i.e., decides on its conventionalization; Schmid 2020).
2. *In* + unmodified noun for time or other context. *In future* has been generally available for a long time in the language, and now we are beginning to hear *in now*, *in past*, and even *in real* (meaning in contrast to something that is fictional or artificial, such as artificial reality, augmented reality, etc.). What will happen? Culture gates.
3. *Because* + noun. We have seen the recent development of *Because* + noun, as in *Because science*. The construction seems to prompt for the meaning that the speaker believes that the noun alone should sufficiently prompt the hearer toward inferring the intended explanation.

So, if someone asks, *Why are you going into the café?*, the answer *Because caffeine* is understood as indicating that the speaker feels that the word *caffeine* is all the speaker needs to be able to figure out the causality, because we all know about caffeine habits. By extension, *Because* + noun can communicate that *if* the speaker knows about the noun (and the frame it evokes), that is enough. *Why are you doing that?* can be answered *Because spouse* since everyone has the frame of marital obligation; if it is answered *Because Pheris*, and speaker and hearer both know that the hearer does not know who or what *Pheris* might be, nonetheless it is being communicated that there exists some meaning paired with the form <Pheris>/[feɹɪs] – whether real, fictional, or imagined – which, if known to the hearer, would be enough for the hearer to understand the whole deal. *Because Pheris* thereby communicates something about the status and power of *Pheris*, even though it does not deliver on the details. And there are related uses of the noun. Q: *What's going on?* A: *Think bankruptcy*. Or *We're talking bankruptcy here*.

A cognitive theory of Construction Grammar is obliged to account at its core for such constant extraordinary creative power and for the sources of cultural constraint on this creativity, including gradients of constraint depending on participants, context, and the shared ground. We see great variety in the kind and degree of constraint on participant uptake depending upon how much constraint is needed to enable communicative collective action. Intimate conversants with deep shared knowledge and experience routinely communicate perfectly with what, for them, are form-meaning pairs and blends of such constructions (despite the fact that outsiders find the performance utterly unintelligible, even though we would all agree that the performers and the outsiders are speaking the same language natively). A member of a family can utter what the whole family recognizes as a quote and understand that the known context of the quote counts as a comment on whatever ground they are in when the quote is performed and in doing so convey meanings unavailable to outsiders. These are not special 'pragmatic' parts of communication but instead are the natural results of the process of blending. Accounting for powerful creativity and the management of creativity for the sake of collective communicative action, including variation in management as needed, is a top requirement of any theory of Construction Grammar.

Blending as a theory of the creation of form-meaning pairs and of their combination into constructs provides, we propose, the path for Construction Grammar to place these fundamental linguistic phenomena at the core of the theory, not as optional peripheral topics.

The authors hasten to emphasize that they hold models lacking these features in high regard for purposes other than building a cognitive theory of Construction Grammar. Natural Language Processing models and gesture models, for example, can be indispensable for the management of big data and for making artificial agents that can interact to an extent with human beings, even though such models lack the essential features of creativity and management of creativity. The authors have spent years advancing these useful models as part of the International Distributed Little Red Hen Lab. But to the extent that any model lacks mechanisms accounting for human-like creativity and culture-like management of creativity, they are not cognitive theories and not suitable as a basis of Construction Grammar.

4.6 Requirement: Multimodality

Human face-to-face communication has always taken place across multiple modalities: through gesture, facial expression, posture, tone of voice, pacing, gaze direction, touch, and words (see, e.g., Kendon 1982, 2004; McNeill 1992, 2000, 2005, 2016). Elaborate multimodal communication is a central and constantly active part of human cognition in science, technology, engineering, mathematics, art, religion, crafts, social interaction, learning, innovation, memory, attention, travel, and all other activities, whether goal-based or not. Cultures invest heavily to support this aspect of human life. Classical cultures emphasized the importance of rhetorical training, and today's world is crowded with novel technologies of multimodal communication, from television to social media, creating an unprecedented trove of digital records. Communication skills involve higher-order cognition, precisely timed movements, delicately modulated sounds, conceiving of the mental states of others from moment to moment, dynamically coordinating with other agents, and a high level of contextual awareness (Duranti & Goodwin 1992; Clark 1996).

From Panini (Sharma 1987–2003) to Chomsky & McGilvray (2012), the systematic study of human communication has been largely focused on the written representation of language: understandably so, as it is difficult to acquire, manage, and analyze data capturing fully multimodal and ecologically valid communicative behavior in specific grounds. Today, however, big multimodal corpora such as the aforementioned Red Hen Lab allow researchers to investigate authentic multimodal communication 'in the wild.' Within Construction Grammar, these new data sources have already spawned new research questions, with many recent publications discussing whether speakers also possess multimodal constructions (i.e., entrenched pairings of verbal+gesture FORM with a conventional MEANING; see Lanwer 2017; Ningelgen & Auer 2017; Schoonjans 2017; Ziem 2017; Zima 2017; Zima & Bergs 2017). We are not denying that this is an interesting area for future research. However, as argued by Hoffmann (2017a) and Turner (2017), before such multimodal constructions can become entrenched, at one point they need to be combined in the working memory of a speaker for the first time. How can people do this? How can they combine spontaneous pairings of gesture and language to express complex meanings that hearers instantaneously understand? Clearly, neither unification nor constraint satisfaction are helpful concepts to explain these multimodal constructs. Conceptual blending, on the other hand, provides a straightforward domain-general explanation for how such multimodal constructs are created and processed (Hoffmann 2017a; Turner 2017).

To know a language, or more generally a communicative system, is to know a relational network of constructions and how they blend to create communicative performances. The crucial part of Construction Grammar is not its analyses of individual constructions in various languages but instead its theory of the creation of form-meaning pairs in the first place and, most important, its theory of the combination of such form-meaning pairs into actual performances. We argue that the cognitive operation that performs this combination is not a computational metaphor such as unification, constraint satisfaction, combination, merge, or feature-structure unification but blending. A theory of such creative formation and combination that relies on non-language-specific cognitive operations is required if Construction Grammar is to be regarded as a cognitive theory of language. Our claim is that blending (Fauconnier & Turner 1996, 2002; Turner 1996; Fauconnier 1997; Turner 2014) is the crucial part of Construction Grammar. In the remainder of this Element, we will illustrate our proposal by showing how blending can be used to account for all types of linguistic combinations, from word-formation over phrasal and clausal phenomena to multimodal communication. Before diving into our in-depth constructional analyses, the next section will briefly survey the main elements of blending.

4.7 Elements of Blending

Cognitive Linguistics analyzes how language derives from and interacts with basic mental operations not exclusive to language. Blending is a basic mental operation, interacting with other basic mental operations such as conceptual mapping, attention, and memory. It plays a pervasive role in language and communication. (See blending.stanford.edu and Turner 2014 for surveys of research.)

Blending theory uses a number of new and old terms (for a full overview, see Fauconnier & Turner [2002] or Turner [2014]):

4.7.1 Conceptual Frame

A frame (Fillmore 1976, 1982) is a small bundle of ideas, stereotypical for a community. We activate parts of frames mentally, often prompted by expressions. Think of a *stockbroker*. We have a mental frame for buying and selling, and a mental frame for the special case of buying and selling securities, particularly stocks and bonds. In the frame, there are roles for the buyer, the seller, what is sold, and the broker who arranges the transaction. When someone says, *I have to call my stockbroker*, everyone can activate the right mental *frame*.

4.7.2 Mental Space

Following Fauconnier (1985), we use the term 'mental space' to mean a small, bundled array of related mental elements that a person activates simultaneously in their working memory. *Mary is queen* prompts for us a mental space A with one element that we take to be a person (presumably) named 'Mary,' and another element *queen*, and a role-value relation between them. If the next sentence is *This is a painting of Mary*, then we activate not just the mental space for *Mary is queen* but also another mental space B, which contains a role *picture* and a particular painting as the value of that role. There is also a representation link between the specific painting in one mental space and the specific person in the other mental space. We can use the word 'Mary' to refer to its counterpart in the painting mental space, and so say, "In the picture, Mary has green eyes." This might be reportable exactly because we think the person Mary has blue eyes. A network of such mental spaces is called, naturally, a 'mental space network' or sometimes a 'mental web.'

4.7.3 Mental Web

A mental web is a set of mental spaces that are activated and connected while one is thinking about a topic. For example, *My brother-in-law, the stockbroker, and his family will travel from San Francisco to Cleveland for Thanksgiving, and we need to learn the time of their arrival so that I can drive down to pick them up* will prompt for many mental spaces, such as a mental space in which I drive my car through complicated holiday traffic, another in which I stop at the appropriate gate at the arrival deck of Cleveland Hopkins International Airport, and on and on. Typically, one cannot hold all these spaces equally active simultaneously in the mind. While we think, we focus on one or another mental space in the mental web. Recently activated mental spaces remain latent and are easier to activate.

4.7.4 Vital Relations

The mental web will have many conceptual connections. The most frequent and important mental connections are the Vital Relations: Time, Space, Identity, Change, Cause-Effect, Part-Whole, Analogy, Disanalogy, Representation, Property, Similarity, Category, Intentionality, and Uniqueness. For example, in the mental web about my picking up my brother-in-law and family at the airport, there will be an element in several of those mental spaces corresponding to *I*, and all of those elements in all of those mental spaces will be connected by *Identity* relations. The pickup at the airport is connected by a *Time* connector to the Thanksgiving feast so that the pickup is suitably prior in time to the mental space in which we all have the feast. But the pickup is also connected by a *Time* connector to the mental space for the speaker in the moment of speaking, so that the pickup is suitably later in time than the moment of speaking. The mental space for that pickup at the airport is linked by a *Space* connector to the home where the feast is held, so that we understand that the airport is at a spatial remove from the home. And so on.

4.7.5 Blend

A blend is a mental space that results from blending mental spaces in a mental web. The blend is not an abstraction, or an analogy, or anything else already named and recognized in common sense, although blending is the basis of the cognitively modern human mind. A blend is a new mental space that contains some elements from different mental spaces in a mental web but which develops a new meaning of its own that is not drawn from those spaces. This new meaning emerges in the blend. Blending is a process that can work over any array of mental spaces in any mental space network. For example, suppose I say, *My brother-in-law, the stockbroker, lives in San Francisco. The stock market opens on the East Coast at 9:30 a.m. but at that moment, it is 6:30 a.m. on the West Coast. So my brother-in-law must awaken every day at about 5 in the morning if he is going to be awake enough to start serious and risky work at 6:30 a.m. If I were my brother-in-law, I would be miserable.* This passage asks us to build a mental space that contains the brother-in-law and a mental space for me, and to connect many mental spaces, many small ideas. One of the spaces it asks us to build mentally is a blended mental space in which there is a man (the one who is miserable) who is imbued with some of what we think about the speaker and some of what we think about the brother-in-law, but only some in each case. This miserable person in the blend has new ideas attached to it. In the blend, I am my brother-in-law, in a way: There is an element in the blend that has the personal identity of the speaker but no longer has the speaker's job. It has the emotions of the speaker but the competence and labor of the brother-in-law. This element is not available from any other space in the mental web. It is unique to the blend. There is a new idea here, one that emerges only in the blend. I-am-my-brother-in-law is a new idea and a very complicated one.

The blend has many elements and properties that are not available from other spaces in the mental web. In the mental spaces that have the brother-in-law (living in San Francisco, arising at 5 a.m., etc.), he is not miserable. In the mental space that has me, I am not miserable. But in the blend, there is a person who is miserable. This person emerges in the blend.

When a mental web contains a blended space, it is often called a 'conceptual integration network,' a 'blending network,' or a 'blending web.'

4.7.6 Projection

The elements and relations that come into the blend from the mental spaces that are blended are called projections. These projections to a blend are always partial (or rather, selective). For example, for *If I were my brother-in-law, I would be miserable,* we project onto the blend the speaker but only a small part of what we know about the speaker. We do not project the speaker's current employment, for example, because then the speaker could not be a stockbroker. We do not project the speaker's currently living in Cleveland. We project from the mental space with the stockbroker brother-in-law the role *stockbroker* and perhaps even *living in San Francisco and accordingly rising every weekday at 5 a.m.*, but not the physical appearance of the brother-in-law, his family relations, and so on. (Otherwise, in the blend, the speaker might have to be his own brother-in-law, which is taboo.)

4.7.7 Emergent Structure in the Blend and in the Mental Web

In the blend, there is a person who is a stockbroker and is miserable. In no other space is it true that anyone is miserable. The misery is *emergent* in the blend. Crucially, there is also a new emergent structure in the mental web outside of the blend. Once we have constructed the mental blend, we realize that the speaker in his own actual reality has an aversion to rising early. This is a new structure we build for the speaker. There is also an emergent structure in the connection between the speaker in his input mental space and the stockbroker in his input mental space, namely a *disanalogy* connection between them having to do with disposition.

4.7.8 Human-Scale

Some bundles of thought are tractable and manageable by the human mind. We call these human-scale. Other bundles of thought are not tractable, either because we cannot grasp them mentally or because they go beyond our mental limits. Political cartoons specialize in providing such human-scale compressions of vast mental webs – as in a cartoon that shows the President of the United States in a suit snatching the rice bowl away from a starving child – and we use this human-scale compression to help us grasp the situation in which a presidential veto of legislation in the United States might affect food supply in far distant lands. Most mental webs laying out what we want to think about would be utterly intractable for us if we could not make a human-scale blend drawing on different mental spaces in the web. The blend then gives us a handy, tractable thing to think about. It helps us access, organize, manipulate, and adjust the mental web in which it now sits. For example, in the vast mental web of thinking about life and possibilities, I can have a compact blend in which I actually am a stockbroker – a simulation that arises through blending, going through the motions, and being miserable. The blend in this case is a human-scale mental simulation. I can now do my best to avoid it or anything like it.

4.7.9 Compression and Expansion

A blend is neither a small abstraction of the mental spaces it blends, nor is it a partial cut-and-paste assembly, because it contains emergent ideas. It is a tight *compression*. It contains much less information than the full mental web it serves. From it, we can reach up to manage and work on the rest of the vast mental web in which it sits.

We use compressed, tight, tractable blends to help us think about larger mental webs. We might say that we carry small, compressed blends with us mentally and unpack or expand them as needed to connect up to what we need to think about. For example, the pithy, compressed little blend with the miserable stockbroker can be used to help the speaker think about any job in a time zone other than the Eastern time zone (GMT-5) and lead him to be vigilant for downsides. In the future, anytime he is offered a new job, he might be vigilant to look for possible burdens that would arise because other members of the work team are not in his time zone.

5 Creative Construction Grammar: Blending in Action

The combination of linguistic elements depends indispensably and fundamentally on conceptual blending – that is the claim we advance in this Element. It follows that the combination of constructions in Construction Grammar must be modeled as an application of the cognitive operation of blending. In this section, we give a sequence of topical illustrations of such modeling and show that, due to the selective projection and emergent projection inherent in constructional combination, the blending approach is superior to other approaches (such as 'simple' combination, constraint satisfaction, coverage, juxtaposition and superimposition, or unification).

More generally, language is a distributed, dynamic system of interaction that evolves, adapts, and transforms to meet the communicative needs of its speakers. One of the most powerful cognitive mechanisms underlying this adaptability is blending, a process by which elements from different conceptual spaces are combined to create new forms, meanings, and performances. Within the framework of Construction Grammar, blending serves as a fundamental tool for creative language use – including very basic, everyday, unremarkable performances whose deep creativity we do not notice because we are habituated to it.

Blending is not a peripheral phenomenon; it is at the heart of Construction Grammar. Whether we are forming new words, constructing idiomatic phrases, or making subtle adjustments in meaning through contextual cues, blending is crucial for forming and using form-meaning pairs and combining them into performances.

5.1 Formal Blends: *Brunch* and the Type

Formal blends represent a fascinating intersection of sound and meaning, where two distinct lexical items are combined to create a new term that encapsulates aspects of both. Consider the term *brunch*, a blend of *breakfast* and *lunch*. This blend is not merely a mechanical combination of two words; it is a creative synthesis that reflects a cultural practice – eating a meal that is neither breakfast nor lunch but something in between.

Blending in this context is a highly productive process, giving rise to a wealth of new terms that capture the nuances of modern life. For instance, *snaccident* – a blend of *snack* and *accident* – refers to the unintended (perhaps mock-unintended) consuming of snacks, often with humorous connotations of guilt or indulgence. The blend works because it succinctly conveys a scenario that many can relate to, where the boundaries between deliberate action and accidental indulgence are blurred.

Another example is *Chunnel*, a blend of *Channel* and *tunnel*, the two lexemes in 'Channel Tunnel,' used to refer to the tunnel that connects England and France by running across what the French call *La Manche*. Here, the blend serves a practical purpose, offering a compact and memorable term for a significant infrastructure project. Similarly, *McJobs* blends *McDonald's* with *jobs* to describe low-paid, low-prospect employment, often in the service industry. The blend carries with it a critical undertone, reflecting societal concerns about the devaluation of labor. Note that a McJob need not have anything to do with McDonald's, hamburgers, fast food of any kind, or even any particular part of the world. Although McDonald's is an input, the projection to the blend from that input is highly selective, with a central emergent meaning in the blend not necessary for either input.

Contemporary culture continues to generate new blends, reflecting evolving social attitudes and trends. *Barbenheimer* – a fusion of *Barbie* and *Oppenheimer* – emerged from the simultaneous summer release of two culturally significant films, creating a term that prompts for not only their themes but also the phenomenon of summer blockbusters (and their effect on the future of going to the movies as opposed to streaming films in one's home). *Yasification*, another recent blend, combines *yas* (a slang expression of enthusiastic approval) with the suffix *-ification*, denoting a process of transformation, often in the context of queer culture. Finally, *unfuckwithable* describes a state of invulnerability, where someone or something is impervious to external negativity or criticism.[7]

For all such cases, constructors and co-constructors clearly have the instantaneous, strong, basic, inexpensive cognitive abilities needed to do sophisticated selective projection and blending to create emergent meaning. In these cases, it is easy to point to the formal blending, the blending of meaning, and the blend of form-meaning pairs. Using such pyrotechnic examples makes pedagogical sense, but it is misleading: These operations are almost always entirely invisible to consciousness. But they are omnipresent in all human communication.

5.2 Compounding: *Jailbait*

Now it might seem obvious that word blendings such as *brunch* require a conceptual blending analysis. However, we argue that all word-formation processes exhibit selective projection and emergent semantic properties and, consequently, are best analyzed using constructional blending. Take one of the most productive word-formation processes in English: N-N compounds. Consider, for instance, the compound *boat house*, which refers to a structure where boats are stored. The blend here involves integrating the concepts of *boat* and *house*, creating a new mental space that encompasses both the physical structure and its intended use. The same process can be seen in *jailhouse*, where the blend integrates the concepts of incarceration and residence, or *doorknob*, where the blend combines the ideas of *door* and *knob* to describe a specific type of hardware.

Land yacht blends the concepts of *land* and *yacht* to describe a large, luxurious car. *Fossil poetry*, a term coined by Ralph Waldo Emerson, blends the concepts of *fossil* and *poetry* to describe language as a repository of historical and cultural layers (much like fossils, which preserve the past in stone).

A *caffeine headache* can be a headache caused by caffeine withdrawal, where the blend integrates the concepts of *caffeine* and *headache* in a way

---

[7] The authors are grateful to the KU Eichstätt-Ingolstadt students of the 2024 class Linguistic Creativity for suggesting *Barbenheimer* and *yasification* as two creative, novel blends.

that emphasizes causality: In the blend, it is the *absence* of caffeine, however, that is the cause. Similar cases of absence emerging in the blend are seen in *money problem, nicotine fit, rice famine*, and so on.

We refer the reader to Fauconnier & Turner (2002) for the fabulous blending complexities and emergent structure for a construct such as 'jailbait.'

5.3 Predication: *The Beach Is Safe*

A common but misguided way of describing the meaning of a sentence like "The beach is safe" is to say that a particular property, *safe*, is predicated of an object, *beach*, by means of the words 'safe' and 'beach.' In this view, "this house is safe" asks us to apply the same particular property, *safe*, to a different object, *house*. So, "safe" just has one meaning, *safe*. It would be straightforward to say "The beach is safe" when we want to let a child play there. And in that situation, it would be equally true that "The child is safe." But now we see that the purported property *safe* attributed to the beach in "The beach is safe" and to the child in "The child is safe" would have to be two different properties – namely, on a first approximation, something like *not potentially harmful* as opposed to *not likely to be harmed*. By the same token, the word 'safe' in the sentence "The beach is safe" would have to contain many properties, enabling such diverse readings as: The beach is legally protected from development, has a statistically low number of drownings, is not a site of violent crime, is owned in such a way that its ownership cannot be taken away from the owner, is a vacation spot that can be proposed without problem to someone (as in a 'safe bet'), and so on. In one sense, 'safe' can mean many different things, but at the same time, there is no subjective apprehension of polysemy in these cases. The details in these cases are actually surprising. They show that in order to make sense of 'safe,' we need to construct a counterfactual situation in which there is a victim, a location, instruments, possessions, and harm to the victim. In the case of the beach that is legally protected, the beach is the victim and the developers do harm to it. In the case of the beach with few drownings, the swimmers are victims and the beach (meaning the water) does harm. In the case of the beach without crime, the vacationer is the victim and the criminals do harm. Alternatively, the owner of the beach can be the victim, or the person to whom we propose vacation spots can be the victim. We see that the noun that 'safe' is applied to can point to many different roles in many different scenarios, not just the role of victim. Consider also "The jewels are safe," "The packaging is safe," or "Drive at a safe speed." The meanings of these predications are not available independent of their blends.

'Safe' is not an exceptional adjective with special semantic properties that set it apart from ordinary adjectives. It turns out that blending is needed quite generally. Even color adjectives, which at first blush look as if they must assign fixed features, turn out to require non-compositional conceptual integration. 'Red pencil' can be taken to mean a pencil whose wood has been painted red on the outside, a pencil that leaves a red mark (the lead is red, or the chemical in the pencil reacts with the paper to produce red, or …), a pencil used to record the activities of the team dressed in red, a pencil smeared with lipstick, not to mention pencils used only for recording deficits. Theories of semantics typically prefer to work with examples like 'black bird' or 'brown cow' since these examples are supposed to be the prototypes of compositionality of meaning, but in fact even these examples illustrate complicated processes of conceptual integration.

5.4 Dative Blends

Ricardo Maldonado (2002, 2016; Flores & Maldonado 2016) has shown that complex dative constructions like applicatives in Mexican Spanish are blends of simpler constructions. For example, the clausal construction involved in *La lluvia me destruyó los zapatos* (The rain destroyed my shoes on me) blends (1) the Transitive construction with a possessed object and (2) the dative schema. Cross-space mapping connects the possessor in the first with the experiencer in the second. Emergent structure in the blend gives the possessor the status of a core participant – an experiencer – coded grammatically by the dative clitic; it conveys personal affectedness from the subjective viewpoint of the possessor. Likewise, in *León le cocinó una paella a Gala* (Leon Cooked Gala a paella), the transitive construction with an effected object (dinner) blends with the dative experiencer (*le…a Gala*) encoding the beneficiary of León's cooking.

5.5 The XYZ Construction: *Geology Is the Kardashians of Science*

Consider the phrase "Geology is the Kardashians of science" (a line from the sitcom *The Big Bang Theory*). Here, the speaker is blending the inputs to suggest (humorously) the celebrity, superficiality, prominence, and popularity of geology among the masses.

Consider as well Turner's (1987) analysis in *Death is the Mother of Beauty* of conceptual connections and their integration. The data therein data consisted of uses of kinship terms, such as 'mother.' The clausal construction involved in "Death is the mother of beauty" is the 'X is the Y of Z,' or XYZ, construction. The XYZ construction has routine everyday use, as in "Paul is the father of Sally." It has been analyzed by Turner (1991, 1998) and Fauconnier & Turner (2002). XYZ contains the 'y-of' construction. A Y-of expression prompts us to perform the following operations:

1. Call up an input space for the relational frame containing y (the element named by Y).
2. Construct a blended space.
3. Project from the element y selectively to create an element y' in the blend.
4. Provide for a w in the input space that will bear an appropriate relationship to y.
5. Project from that element w selectively to create an element w' in the blend.
6. Project the y-w relationship selectively onto y'-w' in the blended space.
7. Provide open-ended connectors from y' and w' in the blend. We expect these connectors to make connections at some point.
8. Expect the open-ended connector from w' in the blend to connect to something picked out by the noun phrase that will follow "of."

For the XYZ construction, we additionally call up a relational frame containing x and z (the elements named by X and Z) and attach the open-ended connector from y' to x and from w' to z. It is possible to compose y-of constructions. That is, what follows the 'of' in the first Y expression can be another Y expression, for as long as we like: "The doctor of the sister of the boss of Hieronymous Bosch." Such a composition of forms asks us to blend several inputs.

5.6 Argument Structure Constructions

Consider "It was like a movie when an older character sacrifices themselves for the good of the journey, like she Gandalfed me" (Taylor Tomlinson 2024, on TikTok), a construct Tomlinson used in a joke to describe how the mother of a boyfriend indirectly warned her not to marry her son. 'Gandalf,' a proper noun, becomes a transitive verb through blending. Again, we want to point out that this example involves more than *Gandalfed* simply filling or being superimposed onto the verb slot of the Transitive construction. It is the selective projection of a particular scene from *The Lord of the Rings: The Fellowship of the Ring* (when Gandalf fights the Balrog so that his companions can flee and, subsequently, seems to die) and takes this fictional heroic sacrifice and likens it to the act of a real person (a boyfriend's mother telling Tomlinson "You know, Taylor, my son's a lot like his father. And if I could go back in time, I don't know that I'd marry his father again."). This, obviously, is another fireworks example: It is part of a stand-up routine and "she Gandalfed me" is used as a punchline intended to make the audience laugh. The utterance entails the blending of the over-the-top fictional sacrifice of Gandalf with the boyfriend's mother's quiet words. In addition, the mother's words invited Tomlinson to blend herself with the mother and her boyfriend with his father and to interpret the mother's statement as an implicit warning not to marry her boyfriend. Only once all these interpretations are projected onto the blended mental space does the "she Gandalfed me" work as a funny punchline.

This kind of blending is not limited to such playful or creative language use; it can also be found in more conventional argument structures. For example, in the sentence *She elbowed her way through the crowd*, the noun *elbow* becomes, in the blend, a verb suitable for one of the Way constructions; in the blend, the elbow becomes an instrument that can be used to create a path that the agent is attempting to traverse. So, even in this example, *elbow* is not unified with or superimposed onto the Way construction. It is blending that allows us to get the desired interpretation (someone using their elbows while pushing through a crowd) and not other potential meanings (such as someone crawling on their elbows through a crowd).[8]

What these examples show is that the combination of words, phrases, and argument structure constructions is not a case of simple addition – it is through blending that we get the constructs just discussed, which exhibit selective projection and emergent meaning properties.

5.7 Multimodal Construction Grammar

It is common to imagine that an organism is driven by its environment. Indeed, it is astounding how life depends upon the ability of an organism to respond to forms it encounters. Even single-celled organisms (like yeast, bacteria, and *Stentor roeseli*) will, on the basis of tiny

---

[8] An anonymous reviewer raises the issue that there are conventional uses of *to elbow* meaning "to dig one's elbow into someone with a view to creating space/forging a path." That is, of course true – but again brings up the problem of regressus ad infinitum: Any construct such as *She elbowed her way through the crowd* can become an entrenched construction after someone hears it for the first time. But how was the construct created in the first place? It required someone to blend the noun *elbow* into the verbal slot of an argument structure construction expressing movement.

encounters with forms, alter their action to find their way to preferred possibilities. We emphasize the partial and fragmentary nature of these encounters with form. Much of the performance of the organism is driven not by full information from the environment but rather by top-down dispositions of the organism. This is true for perception and movement.

At the level of human communication, the organism needs to encounter only the slightest bits of form in order to find its way, imaginatively and creatively, to an interpretation, or even alternative possible interpretations. Imagine you are walking past an airport café and you hear "bad crema": it is quite enough to imagine the scene in which one person is saying "This espresso is no good. Bad crema," and looking at the addressee – perhaps closing the eyes momentarily, or making a palm-down gesture in which the hand, hovering horizontally over the espresso cup, flicks away from the midline of the body. In fact, even if one hears nothing but merely gets a glimpse of the scene, one is likely to come to an interpretation. Understanding is not a matter of absorbing meaning, because all one can perceive is form; and it is not a matter of absorbing full forms, because in fact one needs only partial nudges from fragmentary forms to imagine a full blended form and the meanings they invite one to construct. Seeing someone look at someone else and point through a crowd (or hearing someone say "way through" and point, without seeing the person they are assumed to be addressing) is enough to prompt for meaning. One does not need to hear a full Way construction like "Make your way through the crowd" in order to arrive at the full construction of meaning. Here is a thought experiment: hand someone any text to read aloud and watch them do so. They will add the greatest range of forms that are not at all provided by the text: voice, of course, but also intonation, pauses, body movement, viewpoint direction, face and hand gestures. They can do this because they can simulate mentally the full communication on the basis of partial and fragmentary forms. Accordingly, it is a mistake to argue bluntly that a given form can be a prompt for a meaning only if that form is obligatory in the performance: There are many ways to prompt the hearer to simulate in their imagination forms that are not 'encoded' in the performance. Words, gestures, and forms do not *mean*; they are partial and fragmentary prompts to construct meaning, and they are, in human communication, typically small and simple relative to the massive and complex meanings that human beings construct in response. Speakers must find their way to performing a blend of forms that can prompt hearers to find their way to an interpretation. The imaginative creativity of these interactions is the heart of Construction Grammar.

Multimodal Construction Grammar, if it proposes to be a theory of the processes involved in actual human communication, clearly needs such a theory of creativity. Linguistic constructions deployed in a scene of classic joint attention operate in a multimodal environment. (For a review, see Steen and Turner 2013.) There are long traditions of analyzing constructions as such: In an undergraduate class at UC Berkeley in the 1970s, Charles Fillmore discussed examples such as "If you want to save your life, press the button in front of you right … NOW!" in which the crucial deictic depends upon the prosody and the timing of the utterance, and the pause, which we understand to be part of the utterance from the textual signs of three dots and the rendering of "now" in all caps. We know that to understand the sentence, we must imagine a scene of visual and vocal performance. Although there are many stand-alone gestures that need no vocal accompaniment, co-speech gesture routinely presents visual forms that combine with vocal forms in the construction of a meaning, as when we say "Your keys are here" and point at the keys. Again, one does not need to see the pointing to simulate it mentally if one only hears the utterance but does not see the speaker. Likewise, if one sees someone pointing at the keys while looking at someone else, it is not necessary to hear the utterance to simulate it. Indeed, deictic as a term for a range of linguistic forms comes from the Greek root for 'to point, to show.' Let us sketch some interesting principles for the development of multimodal constructions with a couple of pyrotechnic examples. Using pyrotechnic examples makes it easier to see the creative blending and the multimodality of the constructions but doing so runs the risk of suggesting that blending is typically noticeable and unusual, which is false: Blending is used constantly but in nearly all cases goes without notice.

First consider the clip at http://go.redhenlab.org/mt/05/2016-05-09_YouTube_ifixit_BCJA.mp4 from the YouTube instructional video at https://youtu.be/j1f7wotR_CQ?si=0Ed3tK_ktzYJapAM. The instructor, looking into the camera, says, "If you have any questions about getting the data from your old hard drive to your new hard drive, we made a video for you that covers the process, and we will link to it, right there" and points to and looks at the word 'HERE,' which appears in the blended ground when she points and says "there." The printed word HERE is a form, and we know that its deployment in the blend carries the meaning that clicking on the visible spot directs a web browser to the linked URL. Instead of 'HERE,' the target expression could have been 'LINK' or 'CLICK ME' or 'HELP' or 'THIS IS

WHAT SHE MEANS' or 'BINGO' or a great range of other expressions, all of which would have prompted for this meaning. Accordingly, the form 'HERE' in the multimodal presentation of a web browser prompts for a meaning it does not otherwise have. We know the full network of mental spaces, in which (in addition to the input of classic joint attention) there are inputs of interactive web presentation, of actions the user can perform to cause subsequent web presentations, and so on, and these inputs can create for the construction a standard interpretation, widely recognized by users. Additionally, we know that contrary to the usual form of classic joint attention, the speaker does not actually see the focus of attention where she is pointing and directing her gaze. In the input space of her experience, she does not see it! We are pretty sure that it was added in postproduction by the producers of the tutorial. But in the blend, she absolutely does see it and sees it so well that she directs us to it. We find this usage slightly humorous because without any direct instruction to this effect, we interpret the speaker and producers to be wryly acknowledging the difference between classic joint attention and blended classic joint attention. There is yet another amazing new aspect of this multimodal construction: In classic joint attention, a speaker's saying "The keys are there" does not directly cause the keys to come into existence at the location to which the speaker points and at which the speaker directs their gaze. Under special conditions, this performance could be interpreted as a command directed at the hearer to place the keys there, but the causal chain is complex. But in the blended classic joint attention scenario of the web tutorial, again there is the wry humor of her causing the object to appear by pointing at it. It is like God saying "*fiat lux*." We know, of course, that this means that in the mental network, there is a production crew that will, in post-processing, create a new layer for the video in which the word HERE pops up at the right place in the screen, namely, whatever spot she pointed at. So, at the production level, her pointing and her use of "there" does indeed have causal power for the existence of the focus of joint attention.

The Big Short, a film about the collapse of the USA housing market, presents occasional vignettes about complex financial instruments, including packages of mostly subprime mortgages. The characters in the plot of the film talk about and are involved in such transactions. Then Margot Robbie, an actress who has no character role in the movie, is presented by voice-over as 'Margot Robbie.' We are told that she will explain such financial packages. She is in a bubble bath, sipping champagne served to her by a butler. She looks at the camera, switching the direction of her gaze when the camera selection shifts. When she is finished with her elaborate explanation of financial juggling across wildly complicated investment instruments, which is meant of course to be hilarious from a naked beauty in a bubble bath, since obviously we think a naked bubble bath with champagne is exactly where everyone relaxes from game-theoretic aggression in the trading of financial instruments, she says, "Got it? Good." She sips the champagne, looks into the camera, and says, "Now, fuck off," with great prosody, flashing eyes, a movement of the head, and a raised index finger on the left hand which sweeps away farther left. In classic joint attention, if someone says, "Now, fuck off," with the appropriate co-speech gesture, crucially, it does not mean at all that the hearer will suddenly have no perceptual access to the speaker. But that is exactly what it means, and we know that this is what it means, as a multimodal form for this blended classic joint attention conceptual network. We expect the immediate edit and the disappearance of the image of Margot Robbie, the champagne, and the bubble bath.

There are many other interesting multimodal form-meaning pairs for the multimodal Margot Robbie scene and many other such interesting scenes in the film, including a highly complex but immediately intelligible scene in which Richard Thaler and Selena Gomez, introduced as such, explain the financial instrument called a 'synthetic CDO.' But in that case, the focus of the blended classic joint attention is itself a blend of the system of highly complex and abstract financial transactions and of people making side bets on side bets on side bets at the blackjack table at which Thaler and Gomez are seated.

These are pyrotechnic examples of the multimodality of constructions. But we can see indefinitely many equally creative multimodal packages of form in TV network news. The pyrotechnic example of the instructor pointing to the HERE link that, outside the blended classic joint attention blend, she cannot actually see – because, although it is in the shared ground of the blend, it is not in her studio ground – is an instance of a routine and unnoticed operation in TV broadcast news, in which the anchor says, for example, "We see here now ... ," perhaps even pointing at a spot on the viewer's screen (but of course unseen by the anchor) showing an inset window rolling a video. Outside the blend, the anchor is watching a monitor that the viewer cannot see, and the monitor is presenting the video to the anchor. The anchor does not point at the monitor that they can actually see, but rather in a direction that for the broadcast indicates a spot on the screen carrying the video. The 'here' refers to that spot on the broadcast screen, not to the spot on the monitor that the anchor is actually seeing.

There are many such classes of multimodal construction for blended classic joint attention in TV broadcasts. For example, in classic joint attention, if two people's visual sagittal gazes are parallel as they stand shoulder-to-shoulder, it means that they cannot see each other's eyes. But in the TV news presentation of anchor and reporter in the field, it means exactly that they can see each other, frontally. This multimodal form-meaning pair is entirely standard and recognized as unproblematic for TV broadcast news but impossible for classic joint attention. It is a blended classic joint attention canonical form-meaning pair in opposition to the classic joint attention form-meaning pair.

When the rectangle carrying the video feed of the anchor drops in as an inset from above on the TV broadcast screen, taking its place between two rectangles containing two other people, each of them gazing not into the camera but rather, as we know for the mental network, whatever camera happens to be in whatever studio in which that single person sits, the anchor says, "Joining us now, …" The anchor can introduce the two talking heads and 'say' 'to' 'them,' "Thank you for joining me and the viewers here." This is utterly impossible in a scene of classic joint attention but these multimodal forms have, because of the processes of blending in the scene of communication, straightforward interpretation for this particular blended classic joint attention scene.

In our era of televised presentation, cinema, smartphones, YouTube, Google Hangouts, virtual reality, videoconferencing, and even illustrated literature, the analysis of multimodal constructions is at least as complicated and demanding as the analysis of form-meaning pairs for text, but it is a relatively unexplored arena. We are in an age of new research that will draw on traditions and insights developed over thousands of years, but which has a vast unexplored future of its own. All of this research assumes at its heart a theory of the kind of creativity that makes these communicative performances and interpretations possible. We propose that at present, the only robust candidate for such a theory is the theory of blending, and that blending is the central, domain-general cognitive operation of Creative Construction Grammar.

6 Conclusion

Blending is a basic mental operation constantly and widely deployed in human cognition, almost always entirely below the horizon of observation. Blending is part of the way we think. Far from costly or special, it is, for human beings, omnipresent and constant, central and indispensable to everyday thought, action, and communication. Over time, groups of people create and establish conceptual integration networks and generic integration templates (Pagán Cánovas & Turner 2016), which other members of the group can learn and which come to count as part of a group's abilities and even its identity. Full human language and communication are made possible by these advanced modes of blending. Blending is the central mental operation that makes us able to create constructions, learn constructions, modify constructions, combine constructions, and interpret performances as the result of combining constructions. Additionally, the form-meaning pairs of grammar often have as part of their meaning a set of hints and constraints on blending. Communicative forms do not mean; instead, they prompt human beings to construct meaning. In the last section of this Element, we have illustrated blending in thought and communication by investigating the specifics of a few particular usage events and a few particular constructions. We adduce these examples not for themselves (an entirely different set of examples might have been used to the same effect) but as evidence for – and demonstrations of – our larger claim that theory of communication is a subfield of the theory of blending. Construction Grammar is at its heart a theory of creativity. The status of Construction Grammar as a branch of cognitive science depends upon whether it can offer an adequate theory of creativity. The theory of blending provides Construction Grammar with the indispensable theory of advanced and robust creativity it must have. It is the integral process of the research agenda we call Creative Construction Grammar.

References

Adger, David. 2003. *Core Syntax: A Minimalist Approach*. Oxford: Oxford University Press.

Alexander, James. 2011. Blending in mathematics. *Semiotica* 187: 1–48.

Aristotle. Poetics. 1995. Ed. and trans. S. Halliwell. In Aristotle, vol. 23. Cambridge, MA: Harvard University Press [Loeb].

Atkinson, Elizabeth, et al. 2018. No evidence for recent selection at FOXP2 among diverse human populations. *Cell* 174: 1–12.

Barak, Libby, Afsaneh Fazly & Suzanne Stevenson. 2014. Gradual acquisition of mental state meaning: A computational investigation. *Proceedings of the Annual Meeting of the Cognitive Science Society* 36: 1886–1891.

Bergen, Benjamin K. & Nancy Chang. 2005. Embodied Construction Grammar in simulation-based language understanding. In Jan-Ola Ostman & Mirjam Fried, eds. *Construction Grammars: Cognitive Grounding and Theoretical Extensions*. Amsterdam: John Benjamins, 147–190.

Bergen, Benjamin K. & Nancy Chang. 2013. Embodied Construction Grammar. In Thomas Hoffmann & Graeme Trousdale, eds. *The Oxford Handbook of Construction Grammar*. Oxford: Oxford University Press, 168–190.

Bergs, Alexander. 2018. "Learn the rules like a pro, so you can break them like an artist" (Picasso). Linguistic aberrancy from a constructional perspective. *Anglia* 66,3: 277–293.

Bergs, Alexander. 2019. What, if anything, is linguistic creativity? *Gestalt Theory* 41,2: 1–11.

Bergs, Alexander & Nikola Kompa. 2020. Creativity within and outside the linguistic system. *Cognitive Semiotics* 13,1: 1–21.

Bianchi, Martha Dickinson. 1971. *The Life and Letters of Emily Dickinson*. New York: Biblo & Tannen Publishers.

Boas, Hans C. 2013. Cognitive Construction Grammar. In Thomas Hoffmann & Graeme Trousdale, eds. *The Oxford Handbook of Construction Grammar*. Oxford: Oxford University Press, 233–252.

Boas, Hans C. & Ivan Sag, eds. 2012. *Sign-Based Construction Grammar*. Stanford: CSLI Publications.

Bolinger, Dwight. 1979. To catch a metaphor: *You* as norm. *American Speech* 54: 194–209.

Braine, Martin D. S. 1963. The ontogeny of English phrase structure: The first phrase. *Language* 39: 1–14.

Braine, Martin D. S. 1976. Children's first word combinations. *Monographs of the Society for Research in Child Development* 41,1. Serial No. 164.

Bresnan, Joan & Ronald M. Kaplan. 1982. Introduction: Grammars as mental representations of language. In Joan Bresnan, ed. *The Mental Representation of Grammatical Relations*. Cambridge, MA/London: MIT Press, xvii–lii.

Brunner, Thomas & Thomas Hoffmann. 2020. *The way-construction in World Englishes*. English World-Wide 41,1: 1–36.

Bybee, Joan. 2006. From usage to grammar: The mind's response to repetition. *Language* 82: 711–733.

Bybee, Joan. 2010. *Language, Usage and Cognition*. Cambridge: Cambridge University Press.

Bybee, Joan. 2013. Usage-based theory and exemplar representations of constructions. In Thomas Hoffmann & Graeme Trousdale, eds. *The Oxford Handbook of Construction Grammar*. Oxford: Oxford University Press, 49–69.

Casasanto, Daniel & Gary Lupyan. 2015. All concepts are ad hoc concepts. In Eric Margolis & Stephen Laurence, eds. *The Conceptual Mind: New Directions in the Study of Concepts*. Cambridge: MIT Press, 543–566.

Chomsky, Noam. 1995. *The Minimalist Program*. Cambridge, MA: MIT Press.

Chomsky, Noam. 2021. Minimalism: Where are we now, and where can we hope to go. *Gengo Kenkyu (Journal of the Linguistic Society of Japan)* 160: 1–41.

Chomsky, Noam & James McGilvray. 2012. *The Science of Language*. Cambridge: Cambridge University Press.

Chomsky, Noam, T. Daniel Seely, Robert C. Berwick, Sandiway Fong, M. A. C. Huybregts, Hisatsugu Kitahara, Andrew McInnerney & Yushi Sugimoto. 2023. *Merge and the Strong Minimalist Thesis*. Cambridge: Cambridge University Press.

Clark, Eve V. 2009. *First Language Acquisition*. 2nd ed. Cambridge: Cambridge University Press.

Clark, Herbert H. 1996. *Using Language*. Cambridge: Cambridge University Press.

Coulson, Seana. 2011. Constructing meaning: An interview with Gilles Fauconnier. *Review of Cognitive Linguistics* 9,2: 413–417.

Croft, William. 2001. *Radical Construction Grammar: Syntactic Theory in Typological Perspective*. Oxford: Oxford University Press.

Croft, William. 2013. Radical Construction Grammar. In Thomas Hoffmann & Graeme Trousdale, eds. *The Oxford Handbook of Construction Grammar*. Oxford: Oxford University Press, 211–232.

Culicover, Peter W. & Ray Jackendoff. 1999. The view from the periphery: The English comparative correlative. *Linguistic Inquiry* 30: 543–571.

D'Alembert, Jean Rond. 1767. *Opuscules mathématiques*, Vol. 4, Section 11: Sur les éléments de Géométrie. Paris: Briasson.

Dąbrowska, Ewa & Lieven, Elena. 2005. Towards a lexically specific grammar of children's question constructions. *Cognitive Linguistics* 16,3: 437–474.

Dancygier, Barbara & Eve Sweetser. 2005. *Mental Spaces in Grammar: Conditional Constructions*. Cambridge: Cambridge University Press.

Dancygier, Barbara & Eve Sweetser, eds. 2012. *Viewpoint in Language: A Multimodal Perspectives*. Cambridge: Cambridge University Press.

Deacon, Terrence. 1997. *The Symbolic Species: The Co-evolution of Language and the Human Brain*. London: Penguin.

Demetrius. 1995 [1932]. On style. In Doreen C. Innes, ed. and trans. *Aristotle* Vol. 23 (after translation by William Rhys Roberts). Cambridge, MA: Harvard University Press.

Diessel, Holger. 2006. Demonstratives, joint attention, and the emergence of grammar. *Cognitive Linguistics* 17: 463–489.

Diessel, Holger. 2013. Construction grammar and first language acquisition. In Thomas Hoffmann & Graeme Trousdale, eds. *The Oxford Handbook of Construction Grammar*. Oxford: Oxford University Press, 347–364.

Diessel, Holger. 2015. Usage-based construction grammar. In Eva Dąbrowska & Dagmar Divjak, eds. *Handbook of Cognitive Linguistics*. Berlin: Mouton de Gruyter, 295–321.

Diessel, Holger. 2019. *The Grammar Network: How Linguistic Structure Is Shaped by Language Use*. Cambridge: Cambridge University Press.

Diessel, Holger. 2023. *The Construction: Taxonomies and Networks*. Cambridge: Cambridge University Press.

Diessel, Holger & Michael Tomasello. 2000. The development of relative clauses in spontaneous child speech. *Cognitive Linguistics* 11: 131–151.

Doctorow, Cory. 2023. Amazon Is the Apex Predator of Our Platform Era. *New York Times*, September 27. www.nytimes.com/2023/09/27/opinion/amazon-ftc-antitrust-monopoly.html.

Duranti, Alessandro & Charles Goodwin, eds. 1992. *Rethinking Context: Language as an Interactive Phenomenon*. Cambridge: Cambridge University Press.

Enard, Wolfgang, Molly Przeworski, Simon E. Fisher, Cecilia S. L. Lai, Victor Wiebe, Takashi Kitano, Anthony P. Monaco & Svante Pääbo. 2002. Molecular evolution of *FOXP2*, a gene involved in speech and language. *Nature* 418: 869–872.

Enfield, Nick. 2017. Language in cognition and culture. In Barbara Dancygier, ed. *The Cambridge Handbook of Cognitive Linguistics*. Cambridge: Cambridge University Press, 13–18.

Engel, Cristoph. 2005. *Generating Predictability: Institutional Analysis and Institutional Design*. Cambridge: Cambridge University Press.

Epstein, Samuel D., Hisatsugu Kitahara & T. Daniel Seely 2022. *A Minimalist Theory of Simplest Merge*. New York/London: Routledge.

Everaert, Martin B. H., Marinus A. C. Huybregts, Robert C. Berwick, Ian Tattersall, Andrea Moro & Johan J. Bolhuis. 2017. What is language and how could it have evolved? *Trends in Cognitive Sciences* 21,8: 569–571.

Fauconnier, Gilles. 1985. *Mental Spaces: Aspects of Meaning Construction in Natural Language*. Cambridge, MA: MIT Press.

Fauconnier, Gilles. 1997. *Mappings in Thought and Language*. Cambridge: Cambridge University Press.

Fauconnier, Gilles & Mark Turner. 1994. Conceptual projection and middle spaces. *UCSD Department of Cognitive Science Technical Report 9401*. Available at http://ssrn.com/author=1058129.

Fauconnier, Gilles & Mark Turner. 1996. Blending as a central process of grammar. In Adele Goldberg, ed. *Conceptual Structure, Discourse, and Language*. Stanford: Center for the Study of Language and Information (CSLI), 113–130. [distributed by Cambridge University Press] [Expanded web version 1998, available at http://markturner.org.]

Fauconnier, Gilles & Mark Turner. 1998. Conceptual integration networks. *Cognitive Science* 22,2: 133–187.

Fauconnier, Gilles & Mark Turner. 2002. *The Way We Think: Conceptual Blending and the Mind's Hidden Complexities*. New York: Basic Books.

Fauconnier, Gilles & Mark Turner. 2003. Polysemy and conceptual blending. In Brigitte Nerlich, Vimala Herman, Zazie Todd & David Clarke, eds. *Polysemy: Flexible Patterns of Meaning in Mind and Language*. Berlin/New York: Mouton de Gruyter, 79–94.

Fauconnier, Gilles & Mark Turner. 2008a. Rethinking metaphor. In Ray Gibbs, ed. *Cambridge Handbook of Metaphor and Thought*. New York: Cambridge University Press, 53–66.

Fauconnier, Gilles & Mark Turner. 2008b. The origin of language as a product of the evolution of modern cognition. In Bernard Laks et al., eds. *Origin and Evolution of Languages: Approaches, Models, Paradigms*. London: Equinox, 133–156.

Feldman, Jerome. 2008. *From Molecule to Metaphor: A Neural Theory of Language*. Cambridge, MA: MIT Press.

Fillmore, Charles. 1971. *Santa Cruz Lectures on Deixis*. Bloomington: Indiana University Linguistics Club.

Fillmore, Charles. 1976. Frame semantics and the nature of language. *Annals of the New York Academy of Sciences* 280: 20–32.

Fillmore, Charles. 1982. Frame semantics. In Linguistic Society of Korea, ed. *Linguistics in the Morning Calm*. Seoul: Hanshin Publishing Company, 111–137.

Fillmore, Charles J. 1985. Syntactic intrusions and the notion of grammatical construction. *Berkeley Linguistic Society* 11: 73–86.

Fillmore, Charles J. 1988. The mechanisms of 'Construction Grammar'. *Berkeley Linguistic Society* 14: 35–55.

Fillmore, Charles J. 2013. Berkeley Construction Grammar. In Thomas Hoffmann & Graeme Trousdale, eds. *The Oxford Handbook of Construction Grammar*. Oxford: Oxford University Press, 111–132.

Fillmore, Charles J. & Beryl T. Atkins. 1992. Towards a frame-based organization of the lexicon: The semantics of RISK and its neighbors. In Adrienne Lehrer & Eva Kittay, eds. *Frames, Fields and Contrast: New Essays in Semantics and Lexical Organization*. Hillsdale, NJ: Erlbaum, 75–102.

Fillmore, Charles J. & Paul Kay. 1993. *Construction Grammar*. Berkeley: Ms. Department of Linguistics, University of California.

Fillmore, Charles J. & Paul Kay. 1995. *Construction Grammar*. Berkeley: Ms. Department of Linguistics, University of California.

Fillmore, Charles J., Paul Kay & Mary C. O'Connor. 1988. Regularity and idiomaticity in grammatical constructions: The case of *let alone*. *Language* 64: 501–538.

Flores, Marcela & Maldonado, Ricardo. 2016. Metonimia sintáctica en construcciones de transferencia. *Nueva Revista de Filología Hispánica. El Colegio de México* 63,1: 76–94.

Gazdar, Gerald, Ewan Klein, Geoffrey K. Pullum & Ivan A. Sag. 1985. *Generalized Phrase Structure Grammar*. Cambridge, MA: Harvard University Press.

Gibbs, Raymond W., Jr. 2017. *The Metaphor Wars: Conceptual Metaphors in Human Life*. Cambridge: Cambridge University Press.

Gibbs, Raymond W., Jr. 2018. Words making love together: Dynamics of metaphoric creativity. In Esme Winter-Froemel & Verena Thaler, eds. *Cultures and Traditions of Wordplay and Wordplay Research*. Berlin/Boston: De Gruyter, 23–46.

Gibbs, Raymond W., Jr. 2025. Are creative and routine language really that different? In Sabine Arndt-Lappe & Natalia Filatkina, eds. *Dynamics at the Lexicon-Syntax Interface: Creativity and Routine in Word-Formation and Multi-Word Expressions*. Berlin/Boston: De Gruyter, 43–66.

Goldberg, Adele E. 1995. *Constructions: A Construction Grammar Approach to Argument Structure Constructions*. Chicago: University of Chicago Press.

Goldberg, Adele E. 2003. Constructions: A new theoretical approach to language. *Trends in Cognitive Sciences* 7: 219–224.

Goldberg, Adele E. 2006. *Constructions at Work: The Nature of Generalization in Language*. Oxford: Oxford University Press.

Goldberg, Adele E. 2019. *Explain Me This: Creativity, Competition and the Partial Productivity of Constructions*. Princeton: Princeton University Press.

Grace, Sarah. 2012. "Shortbread, the Little Black Dress of Cookies." bring a little bread, February 3. https://bringalittlebread.blogspot.com/2012/02/shortbread-little-black-dress-of.html.

Hampe, Beate & Doris Schönefeld. 2003. Creative syntax. Iconic principles within the symbolic. In Wolfgang G. Müller & Olga Fischer, eds. *From Sign to Signing. Iconicity in Language and Literature 3*. Amsterdam/Philadelphia: John Benjamins Publishing Company, 243–261.

Harary, Frank. 1969. *Graph Theory*. Reading, MA: Addison-Wesley Publishing Company.

Hartmann, Stefan & Tobias Ungerer. 2024. Attack of the snowclones: A corpus-based analysis of extravagant formulaic patterns. *Journal of Linguistics* 60,3: 599–634.

Herbst, Thomas. 2020. Blending is creative, but blendedness is not: A response to Mark Turner. *Cognitive Semiotics* 13,1: 1–12.

Hills, Thomas T. 2025. *Behavioral Network Science: Language, Mind, and Society*. Cambridge: Cambridge University Press.

Hilpert, Martin. 2019. *Construction Grammar and Its Application to English*. 2nd ed. Edinburgh: Edinburgh University Press.

Hoeksema, Jack & Donna J. Napoli. 2008. Just for the hell of it: A comparison of two taboo-term constructions. *Journal of Linguistics* 44,2: 347–378.

Hoffmann, Thomas. 2017a. Multimodal constructs – multimodal constructions? The role of constructions in the working memory. *Linguistics Vanguard* 3,s1: 1–10.

Hoffmann, Thomas. 2017b. From constructions to Construction Grammar. In Barbara Dancygier, ed. *The Cambridge Handbook of Cognitive Linguistics*. Cambridge: Cambridge University Press, 284–309.
Hoffmann, Thomas. 2018. Creativity and construction grammar: Cognitive and psychological issues. *Zeitschrift für Anglistik und Amerikanistik* 66,3: 259–276.
Hoffmann, Thomas. 2019a. Language and creativity: A construction grammar approach to linguistic creativity. *Linguistics Vanguard* 5,1: 1–8.
Hoffmann, Thomas. 2019b. *English Comparative Correlatives: Diachronic and Synchronic Variation at the Lexicon-Syntax Interface*. Cambridge: Cambridge University Press.
Hoffmann, Thomas. 2020a. Construction grammar and creativity: Evolution, psychology and cognitive science. *Cognitive Semiotics* 13,1: 1–11.
Hoffmann, Thomas, ed. 2020b. Special issue: Construction Grammar and creativity. *Cognitive Semiotics* 13,1.
Hoffmann, Thomas. 2021. *The Cognitive Foundation of Post-colonial Englishes: Construction Grammar as the Cognitive Theory for the Dynamic Model*. (Cambridge Elements in World Englishes). Cambridge: Cambridge University Press.
Hoffmann, Thomas. 2022a. *Construction Grammar: The Structure of English*. Cambridge: Cambridge University Press.
Hoffmann, Thomas. 2022b. Constructionist approaches to creativity. *Yearbook of the German Cognitive Linguistics Association* 10,1: 259–284.
Hoffmann, Thomas. 2024. The 5C model of linguistic creativity: Construction Grammar as a cognitive theory of verbal creativity. *Journal of Foreign Languages and Cultures* 8,1: 139–154.
Hoffmann, Thomas. 2025. *Creativity. Reference Module in Social Sciences*. Elsevier. https://doi.org/10.1016/B978-0-323-95504-1.00588-3.
Hoffmann, Thomas. forthcoming. Cognitive approaches to linguistic creativity. In Xu Wen & Chris Sinha, eds. *The Cambridge Encyclopedia of Cognitive Linguistics*. Cambridge: Cambridge University Press.
Hoffmann, Thomas & Alex Bergs. 2018. A construction grammar approach to genre. *CogniTextes: Revue de l'Association française de linguistique cognitive*. https://doi.org/10.4000/cognitextes.1032.
Hoffmann, Thomas & Graeme Trousdale, eds. 2013. *The Oxford Handbook of Construction Grammar*. Oxford: Oxford University Press.

Hoffmann, Thomas & Graeme Trousdale. 2022. On multiple paths and change in the language network. *Zeitschrift für Anglistik und Amerikanistik* 703: 359–382.

Hudson, Richard A. 2010. *An Introduction to Word Grammar*. Cambridge: Cambridge University Press.

Israel, Michael. 1996. The *Way* constructions grow. In Adele Goldberg, ed. *Conceptual Structure, Discourse, and Language*. Stanford: CSLI, 217–230.

Jacob, François. 1977. Evolution and tinkering. *Science* 196: 1161–1166.

Kemmer, Suzanne & Arie Verhagen. 1994. The Grammar of causatives and the conceptual structure of events. *Cognitive Linguistics* 5,2: 115–156.

Kendon, Adam. 1982. The study of gesture: Some remarks in its history. *Recherches Sémiotiques/Semiotic Inquiry* 2: 45–62.

Kendon, Adam. 2004. *Gesture: Visible Action as Utterance*. Cambridge: Cambridge University Press.

Kleinmintz, Oded M., Tal Ivancovsky & Simone G. Shamay-Tsoory. 2019. The two-fold model of creativity: the neural underpinnings of the generation and evaluation of creative ideas. *Current Opinion in Behavioral Sciences* 27: 131–138.

Lakoff, George. 2008. The neural theory of metaphor. In Raymond Gibbs, Jr., ed. *The Cambridge Handbook of Metaphor and Thought*. Cambridge: Cambridge University Press, 17–38.

Lakoff, George & R. E. Núñez. 2000. *Where Mathematics Comes from: How the Embodied Mind Brings Mathematics into Being*. New York: Basic Books.

Langacker, Ronald W. 1985. Observations and speculations on subjectivity. In John Haiman, ed. *Iconicity in Syntax*. Amsterdam: John Benjamins, 109–150.

Langacker, Ronald W. 1986. An introduction to cognitive grammar. *Cognitive Science* 10: 1–40.

Langacker, Ronald W. 2006. Cognitive Grammar. In Dirk Geeraerts, ed. *Cognitive Linguistics: Basic Readings*. Berlin: Mouton de Gruyter, 29–67.

Langacker, Ronald W. 2008. *Cognitive Grammar: A Basic Introduction*. Oxford: Oxford University Press.

Langacker, Ronald W. 2009. Metonymic grammar. In Klaus-Uwe Panther, Linda L. Thornburg & Antonio Barcelona, eds. *Metonymy and Metaphor in Grammar*. Amsterdam: John Benjamins, 45–71.

Langacker, Ronald W. 2015. Construal. In Ewa Dąbrowska & Dagmar Divjak, eds. *Handbook of Cognitive Linguistics*. Berlin/Boston: De Gruyter Mouton, 120–143.

Langacker, Ronald W. 2017. *Ten Lectures on the Elaboration of Cognitive Grammar*. Leiden/Boston: Brill.

Lanwer, Jens Philipp. 2017. Apposition: A multimodal construction? The multimodality of linguistic constructions in the light of usage-based theory. *Linguistics Vanguard* 3,s1: 1–12.

Lefebvre, Claire. 2004. *Issues in the Study of Pidgin and Creole Languages*. Amsterdam: John Benjamins.

Lewis, C. S. 1936. *The Allegory of Love: A Study in Medieval Tradition*. Oxford. Oxford University Press.

Lieven, Elena, Heike Behrens, Jennifer Speares & Michael Tomasello. 2003. Early syntactic creativity: A usage-based approach. *Journal of Child Language* 30,2: 333–370.

Longinus. 1995 [1932]. On the sublime. In William Hamilton Fyfe & Rev. Donald Russell, trans. *Aristotle*, Vol. 23. Cambridge, MA: Harvard University Press.

Maldonado, Ricardo. 2002. Objective and subjective datives. *Cognitive Linguistics* 13,1: 1–65.

Maldonado, Ricardo. 2016. Metonymic syntactic transfers. Presentation at the 6th UK Cognitive Linguistics Conference. Bangor University. 16 July 2016.

Mandelblit, Nili. 2000. The grammatical marking of conceptual integration: From syntax to morphology. *Cognitive Linguistics* 11,3–4: 197–252.

McCubbins, Mathew D. & Mark Turner. 2013. Concepts of law. *Southern California Law Review* 86,3: 517–572.

McCubbins, Colin H., Mathew D. McCubbins & Mark Turner. 2021. Building a new rationality from the new cognitive neuroscience. In Riccardo Viale, ed. *The Routledge Handbook of Bounded Rationality*. London: Routledge, 409–419.

McNeill, David. 1992. *Hand and Mind: What Gestures Reveal about Thought*. Chicago: University of Chicago Press.

McNeill, David. 2000. Introduction. In David McNeill, ed. *Language and Gesture*. Cambridge: Cambridge University Press, 1–10.

McNeill, David. 2005. *Gesture and Thought*. Chicago: University of Chicago Press.

McNeill, David. 2016. *Why We Gesture: The Surprising Role of Hand Movements in Communication*. Cambridge: Cambridge University Press.

Mesthrie, Raj, Joan Swann, Ana Deumert & William L. Leap. 2000. *Introducing Sociolinguistics*. Edinburgh: Edinburgh University Press.

Michaelis, Laura A. 1994. A case of constructional polysemy in Latin. *Studies in Language* 18: 45–70.

Michaelis, Laura A. 2010. Sign-Based Construction Grammar. In Bernd Heine & Heiko Narrog, eds. *The Oxford Handbook of Linguistic Analysis*. Oxford: Oxford University Press, 155–176.

Michaelis, Laura A. 2013. Sign-Based Construction Grammar. In Thomas Hoffmann & Graeme Trousdale, eds. *The Oxford Handbook of Construction Grammar*. Oxford: Oxford University Press, 133–152.

Michaelis, Laura A. & Knud Lambrecht. 1996. Toward a construction-based model of language function: The case of nominal extraposition. *Language* 72: 215–247.

Müller, Stefan. 2008. *Head-Driven Phrase Structure Grammar: Eine Einführung*. 2nd ed. Tübingen: Stauffenburg Verlag.

Müller, Stefan. 2023. *Grammatical Theory: From Transformational Grammar to Constraint-based Approaches*. Fifth revised and extended edition. Berlin: Language Science Press.

Nettle, Daniel. 2007. *Personality: What Makes You the Way You Are*. Oxford: Oxford University Press.

Nikiforidou, Kiki. 2010. Viewpoint and construction grammar: The case of *past* + now. *Language and Literature* 19,2: 265–284.

Nikiforidou, Kiki. 2012. The constructional underpinnings of viewpoint blends: The *Past + now* in language and literature. In Barbara Dancygier & Eve Sweetser, eds. *Viewpoint in Language: A Multimodal Perspectives*. Cambridge: Cambridge University Press, 177–197.

Ningelgen, Jana & Peter Auer. 2017. Is there a multimodal construction based on non-deictic *so* in German? *Linguistics Vanguard* 3,s1: 1–15.

Núñez, R. E. In preparation. *Humanae Mathematicae*.

Ovando-Tellez, Marcela, Mathias Benedek, Yoed N. Kenett, Thomas Hills, Sarah Bouanane, Matthieu Bernard, Joan Belo, Theophile Bieth & Emmanuelle Volle. 2022. An investigation of the cognitive and neural correlates of semantic memory search related to creative ability. *Communications Biology* 5, Article number: 604 https://doi.org/10.1038/s42003-022-03547-x

Pagán Cánovas, Cristóbal & Mark Turner. 2016. Generic integration templates for fictive communication. In Esther Pascual & Sergeiy Sandler, ed. *The Conversation Frame: Forms and Functions of Fictive Interaction*. Amsterdam: John Benjamins, 45–62.

Perek, Florent. 2016. Using distributional semantics to study syntactic productivity in diachrony: A case study. *Linguistics* 54,1: 149–188.

Pollard, Carl J. & Ivan A. Sag. 1994. *Head-Driven Phrase Structure Grammar*. Chicago: University of Chicago Press.

Rakison, David H. & Chris A. Lawson. 2013. Categorization. In Philip David Zelazo, ed. *The Oxford Handbook of Developmental Psychology*. Vol. 1: Body and Mind. Oxford: Oxford University Press, 591–627.

Recanati, François. 1995. Le présent épistolaire: Une perspective cognitive. *L'Information Grammaticale* 66: 38–44.

Richards, Ivor Armstrong. 1936. *The Philosophy of Rhetoric*. New York: Oxford University Press.

Robertson, Katie. 2023. The Remaking of The Wall Street Journal. *New York Times*, October 5 (updated October 11). www.nytimes.com/2023/10/05/business/media/emma-tucker-wall-street-journal.html.

Rubba, Jo. 1996. Alternate grounds in the interpretation of deictic expressions. In Gilles Fauconnier & Eve Sweetser, eds. *Spaces, Worlds, and Grammar*. Chicago: University of Chicago Press, 227–261.

Sag, Ivan A., Thomas Wasow & Emily M. Bender. 2003. *Syntactic Theory: A Formal Introduction*. 2nd ed. Stanford: CSLI Publications.

Sag, Ivan A., Hans C. Boas, & Paul Kay. 2012. Introducing Sign-Based Construction Grammar. In Hans C. Boas & Ivan Sag, eds. *Sign-Based Construction Grammar*. Stanford: CSLI Publications, 1–30.

Schmid, Hans-Jörg. 2010. Entrenchment, salience, and basic levels. In Dirk Geeraerts & Hubert Cuyckens, eds. *The Oxford Handbook of Cognitive Linguistics*. Oxford: Oxford University Press, 117–138.

Schmid, Hans-Jörg. 2020. *The Dynamics of the Linguistic System: Usage, Conventionalization, and Entrenchment*. Oxford: Oxford University Press.

Schoonjans, Steven. 2017. Multimodal Construction Grammar issues are Construction Grammar issues. *Linguistics Vanguard* 3,s1: 1–8.

Schweppe, Judith & Ralf Rummer. 2014. Attention, working memory, and long-term memory in multimedia learning: An integrated perspective based on process models of working memory. *Educational Psychology Review* 26, 2: 285–306.

Sharma, RamaNath. 1987–2003. *The Aṣṭādhyāyī of Pāṇini*. 6 Vols. New Delhi: Munshiram Manoharlal.

Shibatani, Masayoshi. 1994. An Integrational Approach to Possessor Raising, Ethical Datives, and Adversative Passives. In Susanne Gahl, Andy Dolbey, & Christopher Johnson, eds. *Proceedings of the 20th Annual Meeting of the Berkeley Linguistics Society: General Session*

Dedicated to the Contributions of Charles J. Fillmore. Berkeley: Berkeley Linguistic Society, 461–486.

Shieber, Stuart M. 1986. *An Introduction to Unification-based Approaches to Grammar*. (CSLI Lecture Notes 4). Stanford, CA: CSLI Publications.

Sommerer, Lotte & Freek Van de Velde. 2025. Constructional networks. In Mirjam Fried & Kiki Nikiforidou, eds. *The Cambridge Handbook of Construction Grammar*. Cambridge: Cambridge University Press, 220–246.

Sperber, Dan & Deirdre Wilson. 1995. *Relevance: Communication and Cognition*. 2nd ed. Oxford: Wiley-Blackwell.

Steels, Luc, ed. 2011. *Design Patterns in Fluid Construction Grammar*. Amsterdam: John Benjamins.

Steels, Luc. 2013. Fluid Construction Grammar. In Thomas Hoffmann & Graeme Trousdale, eds. *The Oxford Handbook of Construction Grammar*. Oxford: Oxford University Press, 153–167.

Steen, Francis F. & Mark Turner. 2013. Multimodal Construction Grammar. In Michael Borkent, Barbara Dancygier & Jennifer Hinnell, eds. *Language and the Creative Mind*. Stanford, CA: CSLI Publications, 255–274.

Steen, Francis F. & Mark Turner. 2025. Ahead of the curve, or behind? Teaching students that math is a start-up. In Dragana Martinovic & Marcel Danesi, eds. *Mathematics and Education in an AI Era*. Cham, Switzerland: Springer, 23–36.

Steen, Francis F., Anders Hougaard, Jungseock Joo, Inés Olza, Cristóbal Pagán Cánovas, Anna Pleshakova, Soumya Ray, Peter Uhrig, Javier Valenzuela, Jacek Woźny & Mark Turner. 2018. Toward an infrastructure for data-driven multimodal communication research. *Linguistics Vanguard* 4,1: 1–9.

Sweetser, Eve. 1997. Role and individual readings of change predicates. In Jan Nuyts & Eric Pederson, eds. *Language and Conceptualization*. Oxford: Oxford University Press, 116–136.

Sweetser, Eve. 2012. Introduction: Viewpoint and perspective in language and gesture, from the Ground down. In Barbara Dancygier & Eve Sweetser, eds. *Viewpoint in Language: A Multimodal Perspectives*. Cambridge: Cambridge University Press, 25–46.

Talmy, Leonard. 1986. Decoupling in the semantics of attention and perspective. Presentation at the *12th Annual Meeting of the Berkeley Linguistics Society*, University of California at Berkeley.

Taylor, John R. 2002. *Cognitive Grammar*. Oxford: Oxford University Press.

Tobin, Vera. 2008. *Literary Joint Attention: Social Cognition and the Puzzles of Modernism*. (unpublished dissertation.)

Tobin, Vera. 2010. Grammatical and rhetorical consequences of entrenchment in conceptual blending: Compressions involving change. In Fey Parrill, Vera Tobin & Mark Turner, eds. *Meaning, Form, and Body*. Stanford: CSLI Publications, 329–347.

Tomasello, Michael. 1995. Joint attention as social cognition. In Chris Moore & Philip Dunham, eds. *Joint Attention: Its Origins and Role in Development*. Mahwah, NJ: Lawrence Erlbaum Associates, 103–130.

Tomasello, Michael. 1999. *The Cultural Origins of Human Cognition: An Essay*. Cambridge, MA: Harvard University Press.

Tomasello, Michael. 2003. *Constructing a Language: A Usage-Based Theory of Language Acquisition*. Cambridge, MA: Harvard University Press.

Tomasello, Michael. 2006. Construction Grammar for kids. *Constructions* SV 1–11: 1–23.

Tomasello, Michael. 2014. The ultra-social animal. *European Journal of Social Psychology* 44,3: 187–194.

Tomlinson, Taylor. 2024. But I wasn't looking for a relationship. TikTok, September 28. www.tiktok.com/@taylortomlinsoncomedy/video/7419824372954926382?lang=en.

Trousdale, Graeme. 2018. Creativity parallels between language and music. *Zeitschrift für Anglistik und Amerikanistik* 66,3: 371–380.

Trousdale, Graeme. 2020. Creativity, reuse and regularity in music and language. *Cognitive Semiotics* 13,1: 1–17.

Turner, Mark. 1987. *Death Is the Mother of Beauty: Mind, Metaphor, Criticism*. Chicago: University of Chicago Press.

Turner, Mark. 1991. *Reading Minds: The Study of English in the Age of Cognitive Science*. Princeton, NJ: Princeton University Press.

Turner, Mark. 1996. *The Literary Mind: The Origins of Thought and Language*. New York: Oxford University Press.

Turner, Mark. 1998. Figure. In Cristina Cacciari, Ray Gibbs, Jr., Albert Katz & Mark Turner, eds. *Figurative Language and Thought*. New York: Oxford University Press, 44–87.

Turner, Mark. 2001. Appendix C: Conceptual integration and math. In Mark Turner, ed. *Cognitive Dimensions of Social Science: The Way We Think About Politics, Economics, Law, and Society*. New York: Oxford University Press.

Turner, Mark. 2007. The way we imagine. In Ilona Roth, ed. *Imaginative Minds*. London: Oxford University Press & The British Academy, 213–236.

Turner, Mark. 2008. Frame blending. In Rema Rossini Favretti, ed. *Frames, Corpora, and Knowledge Representation*. Bologna: Bononia University Press, 13–32.

Turner, Mark. 2014. *The Origin of Ideas: Blending, Creativity, and the Human Spark*. New York: Oxford University Press.

Turner, Mark. 2015. Blending in language and communication. In Ewa Dąbrowska & Dagmar Divjak, eds. *Handbook of Cognitive Linguistics*. Berlin: De Gruyter Mouton, 211–232.

Turner, Mark. 2017. Multimodal form-meaning pairs for blended classic joint attention. *Linguistics Vanguard* 3,s1: 1–7.

Turner, Mark. 2018. The role of creativity in multimodal Construction Grammar. *Zeitschrift für Anglistik und Amerikanistik* 66,3: 357–370.

Turner, Mark. 2019. Compression and decompression in mathematics. In Marcel Danesi, ed. *Interdisciplinary Perspectives on Math Cognition*. Cham, Switzerland: Springer, 29–51.

Turner, Mark. 2020. Constructions and creativity. *Cognitive Semiotics* 13,1: 1–18.

Turner, Mark & Gilles Fauconnier. 1995. Conceptual integration and formal expression. *Metaphor and Symbolic Activity* 10,3: 183–204.

Turner, Mark & Gilles Fauconnier. 1999. A mechanism of creativity. *Poetics Today* 20,3: 397–418.

Turner, Mark & Mathew D. McCubbins. 2018. Selves and choices. *Reti, saperi, linguaggi, Italian Journal of Cognitive Sciences* 1: 47–58.

Uhrig, Peter. 2018. I don't want to go all Yoko Ono on you – Creativity and variation in a family of constructions. *Zeitschrift für Anglistik und Amerikanistik* 66,3: 295–308.

Uhrig, Peter. 2020. Creative intentions: The thin line between 'creative' and 'wrong'. *Cognitive Semiotics* 13,1: 1–19.

Ungerer, Tobias & Stefan Hartmann. 2023. *Constructionist Approaches: Past, Present, Future*. (Cambridge Elements in Construction Grammar.) Cambridge: Cambridge University Press.

Van Eecke, Paul & Katrien Beuls. 2018. Exploring the creative potential of Computational Construction Grammar. *Zeitschrift für Anglistik und Amerikanistik* 66,3: 341–355.

Van Trijp, Remi. 2014. Cognitive vs. generative Construction Grammar: The case of coercion and argument structure. *Cognitive Linguistics* 26,4: 613–632.

Velupillai, Viveka. 2015. *Pidgins, Creoles and Mixed Languages: An Introduction*. Amsterdam: John Benjamins.

Yang, Charles, Stephen Crain, Robert C. Berwick, Noam Chomsky & Johan J. Bolhuis. 2017. The growth of language: Universal Grammar, experience, and principles of computation. *Neuroscience & Biobehavioral Reviews* 81,Part B: 103–119.

Ziem, Alexander. 2017. Do we really need a Multimodal Construction Grammar? *Linguistics Vanguard* 3,s1: 1–9.

Zima, Elisabeth. 2017. On the multimodality of [all the way from X PREP Y]. *Linguistics Vanguard* 3,s1: 1–12.

Zima, Elisabeth & Alexander Bergs. 2017. Multimodality and construction grammar. *Linguistics Vanguard* 3,s1: 1–9.

Cambridge Elements

Cognitive Linguistics

Sarah Duffy
Northumbria University

Sarah Duffy is Senior Lecturer in English Language and Linguistics at Northumbria University. She has published primarily on metaphor interpretation and understanding, and her forthcoming monograph for Cambridge University Press (co-authored with Michele Feist) explores *Time, Metaphor, and Language* from a cognitive science perspective. Sarah is Review Editor of the journal, *Language and Cognition*, and Vice President of the UK Cognitive Linguistics Association.

Nick Riches
Newcastle University

Nick Riches is a Senior Lecturer in Speech and Language Pathology at Newcastle University. His work has investigated language and cognitive processes in children and adolescents with autism and developmental language disorders, and he is particularly interested in usage-based accounts of these populations.

Editorial Board

Heng Li, *Southwest University*
John Newman, *University of Alberta (Edmonton)*
Kimberley Pager-McClymont, *University of Huddersfield*
Katie J. Patterson, *Universidad de Granada*
Maria Angeles Ruiz-Moneva, *University of Zaragoza*
Lexi Webster, *Manchester Metropolitan University*
Xu Wen, *Southwest University*

About the Series

Cambridge Elements in Cognitive Linguistics aims to extend the theoretical and methodological boundaries of cognitive linguistics. It will advance and develop established areas of research in the discipline, as well as address areas where it has not traditionally been explored and areas where it has yet to become well-established.

Cambridge Elements

Cognitive Linguistics

Elements in the Series

Language Change and Cognitive Linguistics: Case Studies from the History of Russian
Tore Nesset

Navigating the Realities of Metaphor and Psychotherapy Research
Dennis Tay

The Many Faces of Creativity: Exploring Synaesthesia through a Metaphorical Lens
Sarah Turner and Jeannette Littlemore

Metaphor, Metonymy, the Body and the Environment: An Exploration of the Factors That Shape Emotion-Colour Associations and Their Variation across Cultures
Jeannette Littlemore, Marianna Bolognesi, Nina Julich-Warpakowski, Chung-hong Danny Leung and Paula Pérez Sobrino

Applied Cognitive Linguistics and L2 Instruction
Reyes Llopis-García

Cognitive Linguistics and Language Evolution
Michael Pleyer and Stefan Hartmann

Computational Construction Grammar: A Usage-Based Approach
Jonathan Dunn

Signed Language and Cognitive Grammar
Rocío Martínez, Sara Siyavoshi and Sherman Wilcox

Linguistic Synesthesia: A Meta-analysis
Bodo Winter and Francesca Strik-Lievers

Cognition and Conspiracy Theories
Andreas Musolff

Creative Construction Grammar
Thomas Hoffmann and Mark Turner

A full series listing is available at: www.cambridge.org/ECOG

For EU product safety concerns, contact us at Calle de José Abascal, 56–1º,
28003 Madrid, Spain or eugpsr@cambridge.org.

www.ingramcontent.com/pod-product-compliance
Lightning Source LLC
LaVergne TN
LVHW011853060526
838200LV00054B/4301